VANISHING POINTS

VANISHING POINTS

DICKENS, NARRATIVE, AND
THE SUBJECT OF OMNISCIENCE

AUDREY JAFFE

University of California Press
Berkeley · Los Angeles · Oxford

University of California Press
Berkeley and Los Angeles, California

University of California Press, Ltd.
Oxford, England

© 1991 by
The Regents of the University of California

Library of Congress Cataloging-in-Publication Data
Jaffe, Audrey.
    Vanishing points : Dickens, narrative, and the subject
of omniscience / Audrey Jaffe.
        p.   cm.
    Includes bibliographical references and index.
    ISBN 0-520-06918-8
    1. Dickens, Charles, 1812–1870—Technique.
    2. Omniscience (Theory of knowledge) in literature.
    3. Point of view (Literature)   4. Narration (Rhetoric)
    I. Title.
PR4591.J34   1991
823'.8—dc20   90-15492
                                                    CIP

Printed in the United States of America

9 8 7 6 5 4 3 2 1

The paper used in this publication meets the minimum
requirements of American National Standard for
Information Sciences—Permanence of Paper for Printed
Library Materials, ANSI Z39.48-1984. ∞

Contents

Acknowledgements

My thanks to D. A. Miller, Catherine Gallagher, and Robert Newsom, who were involved with this project from the beginning and contributed valuable insights to it at every stage. Mary Ann O'Farrell, Deborah Dyson, and Peter Schwartz provided consistent emotional and intellectual support as well, and John Kucich, in his capacity as reader for the University of California Press, made revising a more intriguing task than it would otherwise have been. I am also grateful to the University of California Dickens Project for providing me with a forum in which to try out many of these ideas. Ohio State University's College of Humanities helped out with a grant-in-aid, and Jean Gregorek prepared the index.

Chapters 2 and 5 appeared, in somewhat different form, in *Novel* and the *Journal of Narrative Technique*, respectively. They are reprinted here by permission.

.

Note on Editions

I have used the following editions of Dickens's works. Unless otherwise indicated, page references included in the text refer to these editions.

Bleak House (Harmondsworth: Penguin, 1971).

David Copperfield (Harmondsworth: Penguin, 1966).

Dombey and Son (Harmondsworth: Penguin, 1970).

Master Humphrey's Clock and *A Child's History of England* (Oxford: Oxford University Press, 1958).

The Old Curiosity Shop (Harmondsworth: Penguin, 1972).

Our Mutual Friend (Harmondsworth: Penguin, 1971).

Sketches by Boz (Oxford: Oxford University Press, 1957).

The Uncommercial Traveller and *Reprinted Pieces, Etc.* (Oxford: Oxford University Press, 1958).

Introduction

Looking back upon his own poor story, she was its vanishing-point. Every thing in its perspective led to her innocent figure. He had travelled thousands of miles toward it; previous unquiet hopes and doubts had worked themselves out before it; it was the course of the interest of his life; it was the termination of everything that was good and pleasant in it; beyond, there was nothing but mere waste and darkened sky.

—*Little Dorrit*

[T]he very being of writing (the meaning of the labor that constitutes it) is to keep the question Who is speaking? from ever being answered.

—Roland Barthes, *S/Z*

Who is speaking? The question, as Barthes poses it, is raised by classical narrative, in which "the majority of the utterances are assigned an origin . . . either a consciousness (of a character, of the author) or a culture." The classical text is plural, Barthes writes: "an iridescent exchange carried on by multiple voices . . . subject from time to time to a sudden *dissolve*, leaving a gap which enables the utterance to shift from one point of view to another, without warning: the writing is set up across this tonal instability."[1] Barthes's words might also be used to describe narrative omniscience, which comes into being and traces its path through that "dissolve," across tonal instability and different points of view.

1. Roland Barthes, *S/Z*, trans. Richard Miller (New York: Hill and Wang, 1974), pp. 41–42.

1

Missing in such shifts is a circumscribed consciousness: someone speaking. Yet from that absence—as if to compensate for it—often comes a voice so forceful that critics of the novel have traditionally expressed annoyance at its presence. The omniscient narrator has long been identified as an intrusive, authorial voice, interfering with the dramatic representation of character and action and hence with the reader's willing suspension of disbelief. Omniscience is "objectionable," W. J. Harvey wrote of George Eliot, in a comment we may take as representative, "when the author intrudes directly into her fiction either by way of stage directions or of moral commentary"—in other words, we might add, in the nineteenth century.[2] As the term "stage directions" suggests, Harvey here implicitly conceives of the novel as a drama in which only characters should occupy the stage and the director, if a good one, will remain behind the scenes.

In *The Rhetoric of Fiction* (1961), Wayne Booth revealed the weakness of the assumptions underlying such arguments, and in doing so underscored what he considered the author's ubiquity. If we were to demand that all signs of the author's presence be eliminated from the literary work, Booth argued, we would soon be left with nothing. For Booth, the author is always present in the work and "can never choose to disappear."[3] But linguistic and literary theory have since called the necessity and even the possibility of locating personality or presence in writing into question. Emile Benveniste points to the shifting quality of such categories as the first-person pronoun, arguing that it refers to a position but not a person. John Sturrock writes that the reality of the author "has had to be sacrificed because language is an objective, collective system

---

2. W. J. Harvey, *The Art of George Eliot* (London: Chatto and Windus, 1961), p. 69. Throughout his chapter on Eliot's omniscience, Harvey balances his interest in Eliot's particular use of omniscience against his sense of the need for critical abstractions. Harvey's response to Eliot's omniscience may also be informed by his sense that male authors handle this technique better than female ones. See my conclusion for a discussion of this issue.

3. Wayne Booth, *The Rhetoric of Fiction* (Chicago: University of Chicago Press, 1961), p. 20.

which we can only use, never expropriate. The real 'I' is thus debarred from ever putting in an appearance: 'I cannot *write* myself. What is this me that might write itself?' " And in *Structuralist Poetics* Jonathan Culler objects strongly to what he calls the "naturalization" of the narrator, the tendency to treat the narrator as a character or to assign a narrator's observations to a character in the text. Critics can't stand the idea of impersonality, Culler asserts, and the business of identifying narrators provides them with an easy way of resolving inconsistencies—thereby "humanizing writing and making personality the focal point of the text." For Culler, narrative reflects the impersonality of language itself; it is simply "writing."[4]

Thus, if earlier critics tended to find the "authorial" narrator's voice intrusive, for more recent critics that voice hardly exists at all. Or rather, it refers not to individuals but to institutions. Giving the discussion about the personality or impersonality of the narrative voice an explicitly social focus, critics have elaborated the implications for the novel of Michel Foucault's analyses of disciplinary institutions, aligning the omniscient narrator with the invisible observer at the center of Jeremy Bentham's Panopticon. According to these readings, the invisible narrator is an agent of disciplinary society, and even the term "narrator," as D. A. Miller writes, falsely represents "a technique that, never identified with a *person*, institutes a faceless and multilateral regard."[5]

The novel critic must now choose, it seems, between treating the omniscient narrator as presence or personification, or as impersonal technique. But there is an alternative to consid-

4. Emile Benveniste, *Problems of General Linguistics*, trans. M. Meek (Coral Gables: University of Miami Press, 1971), p. 225; John Sturrock, "Roland Barthes," in John Sturrock, ed., *Structuralism and Since: From Lévi-Strauss to Derrida* (New York: Oxford University Press, 1979), p. 77, quoting Roland Barthes, *A Lover's Discourse* (New York: Hill and Wang, 1978); and Jonathan Culler, *Structuralist Poetics* (Ithaca: Cornell University Press, 1975), p. 201.

5. D. A. Miller, *The Novel and the Police* (Berkeley and Los Angeles: University of California Press, 1987), p. 24. See also Michel Foucault, *Discipline and Punish*, trans. Alan Sheridan (New York: Vintage, 1979), and Jonathan Arac, *Commissioned Spirits: The Shaping of Social Motion in Dickens, Carlyle, Melville, and Hawthorne* (New Brunswick, N.J.: Rutgers University Press, 1979).

ering the absence of a characterized narrator either as an "implied" author, a device through which we form a personal relationship with the author; or as a threatening lack that needs to be filled by some form of character; or simply as "writing," requiring us to do away with the mediating presence of the author or narrator altogether. Rather than naturalize omniscience, we can interest ourselves precisely in the way in which it naturalizes or refuses to naturalize itself—at times speaking "personally," at times representing abstract knowledge (what the reader already knows or needs to know). What we call omniscience can be located, that is, not in presence or absence, but in the tension between the two—between a voice that implies presence and the lack of any character to attach it to, between a narratorial configuration that refuses character and the characters it requires to define itself. And rather than claim that omniscience speaks from this or that character's point of view, we might ask what character signifies, as a construct the narrator's voice attributes to others but avoids itself.

Omniscience is traditionally considered "not a descriptive term so much as a definition based on the presumed analogy between the novelist as creator and the Creator of the cosmos, an omniscient God."[6] Narrative theorists such as Shlomith Rimmon-Kenan, Gérard Genette, Dorrit Cohn, and Seymour Chatman have filled out some of the details of this analogy. In Rimmon-Kenan's words, for instance, "the characteristics connoted by it are . . . familiarity, in principle, with the characters' innermost thoughts and feelings; knowledge of past, present, and future; presence in locations where characters are supposed to be unaccompanied . . . and knowledge of what happens in several places at the same time."[7] Histories of the novel depend on a similar account. Discussions of the

6. Robert Scholes and Robert Kellogg, *The Nature of Narrative* (New York: Oxford University Press, 1966), p. 272.

7. Shlomith Rimmon-Kenan, *Narrative Fiction: Contemporary Poetics* (London: Methuen, 1983), p. 95. Seymour Chatman opposes omniscience to limitation "in terms of the capacity to enter characters' consciousnesses"; see his *Story and Discourse* (Ithaca: Cornell University Press, 1978), p. 212.

transition from the Victorian to the modern novel almost always rely on the idea of the disappearance of the omniscient narrator, defined as absolute authority or knowledge. Implicitly or explicitly invoking the analogy between the narrator and an omniscient God, such discussions assume a certainty out of which modernism's uncertainty emerges. And although J. Hillis Miller, for instance, has argued that for a number of writers "the nineteenth and twentieth centuries seem . . . a time when God is no more present," the standard view of the difference between twentieth-century fiction and fiction of the previous two centuries has hardly changed since David Daiches characterized it in terms of "the drying up of traditional sources of value and the consequent decay of uniform belief."[8]

The assertion of knowledge and authority, however, does not necessarily reflect their secure possession. My argument about omniscience resembles a case Marshall Brown has made for realism. When realism emerges into consciousness as a subject of discourse or deliberate technique, Brown argues, the assumptions underlying it are no longer being taken for granted. "[T]he point of historical articulation is also the point of disarticulation," he writes.[9] Omnisciently narrated novels of the nineteenth-century (and I refer here generally to the work of canonical novelists, such as Dickens, Eliot, and Thackeray) are notably ambitious in scope, taking as their projects the representation of entire social worlds from an external perspective as well as from within the consciousness of characters. The explicit and implicit insistence on narratorial knowledge this project involves—the delineation, for instance, of sharp epistemological distinctions between narrator and char-

8. J. Hillis Miller, *The Disappearance of God* (Cambridge: Harvard University Press, 1963), p. 2; David Daiches, *The Novel and the Modern World* (Chicago: University of Chicago Press, 1939), p. 7. See also Alan Friedman, *The Turn of the Novel* (New York: Oxford University Press, 1968), and George Levine, *The Boundaries of Fiction: Carlyle, Macauley, Newman* (Princeton: Princeton University Press, 1968), p. 75.

9. Marshall Brown, "The Logic of Realism: A Hegelian Approach," *PMLA* 96 (1981): 224.

acter—suggests that omniscience is not so much evidence for the possession of knowledge as an emphatic display of knowledge, a display, precisely, of what is not being taken for granted.

The qualities Rimmon-Kenan cites as constitutive of omniscience depend, in order for us to perceive them at all, on their opposites. Knowledge appears to us only in opposition to its absence; an effect of unboundedness is created in contrast to one of limitation. Thus when omniscient narration demonstrates the ability to transcend the boundaries that confine characters, it must construct the very boundaries it displays itself transcending. Rather than being a static condition, then, the evidence of an unquestioned authority, omniscience is the inscription of a series of oppositions which mark a difference between describer and objects of description: oppositions between sympathy and irony, involvement and distance, privacy and publicity, character and narrator, self and other—and, most generally, the assertion of narratorial knowledge and its absence in characters. Omniscience is an effect of narrative strategies, continually—in spite of and in distinct contrast to its invisibility—making itself felt.[10]

Omniscience in general, I argue here, is a fantasy: of unlimited knowledge and mobility; of transcending the boundaries imposed by physical being and by an ideology of unitary identity. It not only dominates nineteenth-century narrative but takes a particularly contradictory and complex form there because it expresses both structurally and thematically tensions present within Victorian culture—tensions about the relationship between knowledge and authority, the separation of public and private spheres, and the nature and role of individual sympathy in a bureaucratic age. Though it is the

---

10. For the most part (when not too awkward) I have used the impersonal "it" to designate omniscience in general, and the masculine "he" when describing Dickens's omniscience in particular. I do not want to claim that a narrator's and author's genders must be identical, nor do I argue that omniscient narration is in every case implicitly male. My use of the masculine form is, however, predicated on the idea that Dickens's omniscience implicitly participates in and reinforces masculine structures of meaning.

period's dominant novelistic form, omniscience was not invented by the nineteenth century, nor do the claims I make for it necessarily apply only to its nineteenth-century forms. Rather, my argument presupposes that narrative forms are cultural forms, expressions of historically specific emotional and epistemological characteristics.[11] Nor does this reading depend upon locating somewhere in the history of the novel an alternative, secure omniscience. Such an omniscience is, I believe, a fantasy created by practical critics and narrative theorists, who have often faulted novelists for their failure to achieve it.

This study links what I refer to as Dickens's fantasy of omniscience with an articulation of the narrative strategies employed in his novels and sketches to produce an effect of omniscience. A rereading of Dickens, it is also a rereading of narrative conventions, one which calls into question traditional, well-protected definitions of and distinctions between such elements as person, plot, and theme. For if omniscience is understood to be a fantasy about knowledge, then what has been regarded as a purely structural concern with locating and defining levels of knowledge is also, necessarily, the subject of the omnisciently narrated novel. As Ross Chambers points out, to narrate is, etymologically, to be the one who knows, and that some entity knows or appears to know is a matter of content no less than of form.[12] In considering omniscience to be the subject of narrative as well as a description of its form, this study demonstrates how omniscient narration's inherent structural tensions break down distinctions between ideas such as "structure," "plot," and "theme," and problematize commonly accepted differences between first- and third-person.

---

11. For instance, John Bender finds tensions between personified narration and impersonal authority in *The Vicar of Wakefield*, linking them to changes in the penal system: "Prison Reform and the Sentence of Narration in *The Vicar of Wakefield*," in Felicity Nussbaum and Laura Brown, eds., *The New Eighteenth Century* (New York: Methuen, 1987), pp. 168–88.

12. See Ross Chambers, *Story and Situation: Narrative Seduction and the Power of Fiction* (Minneapolis: University of Minnesota, 1984), p. 50.

The predominance of omniscient narration in nineteenth-century fiction has an obvious affinity with the period's enthusiasm for scientific objectivity and for the accumulation of knowledge—the collection and distribution of facts—in general. Indeed, the tremendously increased production of printed literature engendered by the industrial revolution, along with such contemporaneous developments as the statistical movement, created the sense that the production of knowledge was itself an industry.[13] As information, in the form of statistics and parliamentary reports, was collected by various administrative bodies and widely disseminated in newspapers and journals, several effects significant for an interpretation of nineteenth-century omniscience occurred. First, the possession of such information began to seem in itself a form of power.[14] Second, such knowledge seemed to take an impersonal form, emanating not from individuals but from commissions, traceable to no place and no person in particular. The scientific model took for granted the possibility of objectivity, of clear and precise vision—of, as Matthew Arnold famously put it, "disinterest," the subordination of personal interest to an ideal of concrete and correct information. And finally, in the context of this rapid production, dissemination, and what we might call objectification of knowledge, the boundaries of knowledge were felt to be continually expanding. The "minimal standard of an educated man," according to a definition offered by Augustus De Morgan, was that he know "something of everything and everything of something."[15] The period's obsession with counting and classifying expresses the same anxiety about the constitution and possession of knowledge that, I argue, omniscient narration

13. See Richard Altick, *The English Common Reader* (Chicago: University of Chicago Press, 1957) on the proliferation of printed matter and the growth of the reading public in England.
14. For a discussion of information as power, see Alexander Welsh, *George Eliot and Blackmail* (Cambridge: Harvard University Press, 1985), ch. 3.
15. Augustus De Morgan, quoted by S. S. Schweber in "Scientists as Intellectuals: The Early Victorians," in James Paradis and Thomas Postlewait, eds., *Victorian Science and Victorian Values: Literary Perspectives* (New Brunswick, N.J.: Rutgers University Press, 1985), p. 3.

does. As novels work to achieve the effect of reproducing a complex social whole, they simultaneously assert their ability to manage a vast, potentially unmanageable amount of information.

If omniscience is linked to scientific objectivity and public knowledge, however, it is at its most characteristic when demonstrating its knowledge of what (as Dickens's narrators frequently comment) "no one" knows: what goes on in private, within the family, and in the minds of characters. Unseen observation grants narrators a power and mobility that characters do not possess. It requires an invasion of privacy best accomplished if the narrator is present, as Rimmon-Kenan put it in the definition cited above, "in locations where characters are supposed to be unaccompanied." The boundary omniscient narration most significantly and problematically transgresses in the nineteenth century is that between public and private spheres; not surprisingly, this is the boundary it also secures. For it is precisely by invading privacy that omniscience defines the boundaries of privacy for nineteenth-century readers. While expressing a distinctively Victorian anxiety about knowledge, then, omniscient narration is also in the business of constructing the knowledge that shapes Victorian ideologies, affirming for readers what appear to be truths of character and of private life. Omniscient narration thus serves both "personal" and "impersonal" functions and projects both individual and collective fantasies. A subject's self-effacement enables his or her participation in a larger, cultural gaze, while the construction of others as subjects enables a narrator to imagine, at least temporarily, eluding that gaze.

Dickens expressed interest in the relationship between personal and impersonal knowledge early in his career. Indeed, the question of whether abstract knowledge could be presented in personal form was at the center of his conception for the journal *Household Words*. He wanted *Household Words* to personalize—to domesticate, as its title suggests—the vast machinery of the industrial age by presenting scientific and statistical information informally, to lead the reader "into new associations with the Power that bears him onward."[16] Thus when the journal discusses the question of the purity of London's water—a topic whose exposition involves statistics from blue books, data on the water's composition, a detailed account of the machinery involved in purification, and a description of the route the water takes from factory to home—it encloses this material in a dialogue between two friends, who decide to approach the subject by means of "ocular demonstration": a visit to the waterworks.[17]

But it may prove difficult to enter into a personal relationship with the "Power" that bears you onward. As Richard Maxwell points out, "The very idea of omniscience is difficult to associate with human feeling."[18] Statistics may emerge from the mouths of observers, and one may even have those observers taste the water, without altering a reader's sense that the information presented is ultimately impersonal and abstract. *Household Words* did not succeed in its goal of personalizing information. But the work that preceded and followed it—from the *Sketches'* ambivalent narrative persona to the divided narration of *Bleak House* and beyond—reveals a similar interest in negotiating a relationship between the impersonal and the personal.

Just as Dickens explored this tension, so too have his readers often felt it necessary to decide the personality or impersonality of his narrative voice, some insisting on the materiality and omnipresent personality of that voice, others failing to see in it any "person" whatsoever.[19] And while many readers have agreed that Dickens is insistently present in his works, some have also felt the need to account for a narratorial voice at times so distant as to amount "almost to the viewpoint of a god . . . inducing fantasies of omniscience and omnipo-

16. "Preliminary Word," *Household Words*, vol. 1, 30 March 1850, p. 1.

17. "The Troubled Water Question," *Household Words*, vol. 1, 13 April 1850.

18. Richard Maxwell, "Dickens's Omniscience," *ELH* 46 (1979): 293.

19. For the first view, see Robert Garis, *The Dickens Theatre* (Oxford: Clarendon Press, 1967); for the second, Taylor Stoehr, *Dickens: The Dreamer's Stance* (Ithaca: Cornell University Press, 1965), and Elizabeth Ermarth, *Realism and Consensus in the English Novel* (Princeton: Princeton University Press, 1983).

tence."[20] The idiosyncratic narrative voice that readers perceive as distinctively Dickensian also manifests itself as a distant and knowing one. Moreover, his personified narrators, such as Boz, David Copperfield, and Esther Summerson, often remain peculiarly disembodied. But this tension between personality and impersonality is constitutive of omniscient narration as I have described it. Indeed, we might say that insofar as "Dickens" is present to us in the novels, he is divided between the narrator's mobility and freedom and the character's bound and embodied condition. And the former constructs itself in relation to, and depends upon, the latter.

A similar tension between presence and absence, or personality and impersonality, appears in the structure of the panopticon, invoked by novel theorists ever since the appearance of Foucault's *Discipline and Punish* as a metaphor for novelistic omniscience and for the novel's deployment of disciplinary power. According to Foucault's logic, it does not matter who is inside, or even that anyone be inside, the panoptic tower; the perpetuation of discipline requires only the individual subject's internalization of the idea of surveillance. But discipline nevertheless has its agents. There is a face inside the panopticon, just as there is an interested author behind omniscience's disinterest. The inculcation of a feeling of being constantly under surveillance depends, Bentham explains, on actual surveillance: "For the greatest proportion of time possible, each man should actually *be* under inspection."[21] Though the panoptic system depends on the internalization of the gaze, that gaze can be internalized only if it is first, and often, made visible. There is thus a certain poetic satisfaction in the way Bentham describes his personal investment in the Panopticon project: "By every tie I could devise, my own fate had been bound up by me with theirs. . . . Recluse by inclination, popular at the call of duty, I did not shun the light—I courted it. Self-devoted to the task of unre-

20. H. P. Sucksmith, *The Narrative Art of Charles Dickens* (Oxford: Clarendon Press, 1970), pp. 157–58.

21. "Panopticon; or, the Inspection-House," in *The Works of Jeremy Bentham* (New York: Russell and Russell, 1962), vol. 4, p. 44.

mitting inspection, it would have been a reward to me, not a punishment, to be as unremittingly inspected" (177). Inviting—indeed, desiring—surveillance, the observer acknowledges his implication in the system he oversees. Rather than being taken for granted, the system's power must repeatedly be constructed and displayed, both to the prisoners and to the general public. Like the secret weapon in Stanley Kubrick's *Dr. Strangelove*, unseen observation can function as a disciplinary strategy only if those subjected to it are made aware of it.

The inspector's or omniscient narrator's difference from those he observes is an effect of his position in relation to them—and the latter's insistence on that difference betrays anxiety about the potential similarity between observer and observed. At once refusing the boundaries of character but defining itself by manufacturing those boundaries, omniscient narration reflects a concern about character's limitations and represents an attempt to transcend these limitations by becoming a non-character, a presence but not an objectifiable participant. Even though the subject of omniscient narration has gone into hiding, however, the positions of subject and object remain mutually dependent. The relationship between narrator and character is in its basic structure a projective one. A fantasy of knowledge, mobility, and authority, the omniscient narrator can come into being only in contrast to limitation, which is constructed in the form of character. Omniscience possesses the mobility and freedom that characters do not, but more precisely it possesses that mobility and freedom in relation to and at the expense of what it constructs as characters. Rather than signifying pure absence, then, omniscience is an evasion of presence and its consequences; rather than being a manifestation of authorial consciousness, it is an effect of narrative strategies which evoke but also attempt to exceed consciousness.[22] Present everywhere but free of sur-

---

22. For discussions of omniscient narration as "general" or "collective consciousness, see J. Hillis Miller, *The Forms of Victorian Fiction* (Notre Dame, Ind.: Notre Dame University Press, 1968), pp. 53–90, and Ermarth, *Realism and Consensus in the English Novel*, pp. 65–92.

veillance, the focus of attention but not of gazes, the omniscient narrator is subject but not object of the text. But by collapsing the difference between subject and object, narrator and narrated—by speaking about what refuses to speak about itself—we can begin to elaborate what the boundedness of character signifies: what is at stake in the narrator's refusal of character.

At one point in Dickens's *Little Dorrit*, the character Miss Wade makes the following comment: "In our course through life we shall meet the people who are coming to meet *us*, from many strange places and by many strange roads . . . and what it is set to us to do to them, and what it is set to them to do to us, will all be done" (63). What is striking about this remark is, on the other hand, its resemblance to an authorial point of view and, on the other, its hostility. Not only is all action predetermined, but action is antagonistic; the novel's characters, imagined here as travelers, will not simply meet and affect one another, but they are "set" to "do to" one another. Even if we take this remark simply as an expression of Miss Wade's own hostility, we can see that it evokes an omniscient narrator's relation to characters. The characters, embedded in the novel's plot, do not know what lies ahead, being but objects of a narrator's machinations, participants in a structure they cannot perceive. From this point of view, a narrator's relation to characters inevitably involves a demonstration of knowledge and an element of aggression.

The difference between omniscient narrator and character is inscribed in the nineteenth-century novel, and emphatically in Dickens's novels, as a difference in representation: characters are constructed as psychological entities, with identifiable patterns of speech and behavior, and as physical entities, distinguished by bodily features and details of clothing. Such representation, I argue, signifies epistemological boundaries as well. The omniscient narrator's knowledge thus importantly depends on his immateriality or invisibility: the narrator remains indeterminate, exempt from the constructedness of character. (And even when a narrator is also a character, as I discuss below—a Boz, David Copperfield, or Esther Summerson—as narrator he or she exceeds the boundaries of those characters represented, and exceeds them—like an omniscient narrator—*as* a result of representing them.) It is thus essential to recognize that character in the nineteenth-century novel is above all a material construct—that it is, to use a phrase of Baudrillard's, "clothed with marks."[23]

The significance of such an idea for a discussion of Dickens is immediately apparent. Dickens's characters are famously marked: eccentric in appearance and character, doomed in general to repeat the same phrases, whistle the same tunes, twitch the same twitches throughout their lives as characters, even if and when they exhibit a capacity for change. Such habitual behavior, however, is only the logical endpoint of the way novelistic character tends to be defined in general. Character, as Rimmon-Kenan points out, emerges from repetition.[24] The difference between narrator and character is the difference between marked and unmarked—or, to put it in slightly different terms, markedness is the sign of the narrator's projection of difference onto character. Character in Dickens is the narrator displaced and disfigured: projected outward and made visible.[25]

But Dickens's works also contain relatively unmarked characters, figures such as John Harmon and Florence Dombey, whose representations are less firmly inscribed than those of other characters and between whom and the reader there is scarcely any boundary. Both these figures and Dickens's first-person narrators might be called Asmodean participant-narrators, with reference to the invisible demon Asmodeus of Alain LeSage's *Le diable boiteux*—the demon who flies over houses

23. Jean Baudrillard, *For a Critique of the Political Economy of the Sign*, trans. Charles Levin (St. Louis: Telos Press, 1981), p. 95.

24. Rimmon-Kenan, *Narrative Fiction*, ch. 3.

25. Sander Gilman discusses the same structure in terms of the production of stereotypes: "The mental representation of difference is but the projection of the tension between control and its loss present within every individual in every group. That tension produces an anxiety that is given shape as the Other." Gilman explains that, as the projection of anxiety outside the self, difference appears as pathology. See *Difference and Pathology: Stereotypes of Sexuality, Race, and Madness* (Ithaca: Cornell University Press, 1985), p. 24.

and sees through their rooftops.[26] Imagining such a figure as a unifying device for *Household Words*, Dickens described it thus to Forster: "I want to suppose a certain SHADOW, which may go into any place. . . . a kind of semi-omniscient, omnipresent, intangible creature. . . . I want to open the first number with this Shadow's account of himself and his family. I want to have all the correspondence addressed to him. I want him to issue his warnings from time to time, that he is going to fall on such a subject; or to expose such and such a piece of humbug; or that he may be expected shortly in such and such a place." The shadow would, as Dickens put it, "loom as a fanciful thing all over London. . . . a sort of previously unthought of Power going about."[27]

Omniscience, I have suggested, is an appropriate narrative mode for the age that developed statistical science, producing vast quantities of information attributable to impersonal agencies rather than to individuals. "Semi-omniscience," however, more accurately describes these knowledge-producing bodies, which can never succeed in fully capturing the subjects they set out to describe, and whose own interests are revealed in their ostensibly objective descriptions. And semi-omniscience also describes Dickens's Asmodean narrators and characters as they hover between presence and absence, providing a locus for reader identification while remaining diffuse enough to evade the fixed characterizations assigned to other figures. The term suggests the tension within the idea of omniscience as Dickens construes it. The "semi" in "semi-omniscient" presumably points to the shadow's human qualities: to what, for an omniscient narrator, would be limitations. It refers to a figure who has a local habitation, if not a name, and answers

26. Discussions of Asmodeus tend to concentrate on Dickens's attempt to transform a "demon" into a "good spirit." See Peter Garrett, *The Victorian Multiplot Novel* (New Haven: Yale University Press, 1980), and Maxwell, "Dickens's Omniscience."

27. John Forster, *Life of Charles Dickens* (London: Chapman and Hall, 1872), II: 419–20; subsequent references to this work are included in the text. Note that despite Dickens's later use of similar female figures, the shadow he imagined for *Household Words* is explicitly male.

his own correspondence. But these qualities conflict with the rest of the fantasy—the idea, for example, of the shadow "loom[ing] . . . all over London," issuing warnings that he may shortly appear. And they are at odds with the idea of a wide-ranging invisible presence whose knowledge seems potentially unlimited. What kind of knowledge would the shadow deny himself, in order to be semi-omniscient? The phrase describes a tension between a desire for personal knowledge gained through sympathetic identification (to be a shadow is necessarily to be dependent on those one observes, to take one's form from them) and a desire for impersonal knowledge acquired through surveillance. The shadow combines these, but with difficulty: he is a figure of contradictions.

The Asmodean figures discussed in the following chapters—Boz, Humphrey, Florence Dombey, David Copperfield, Esther Summerson, and John Harmon—are what Genette has called "focalized" characters, though the term suggests too strongly that we can see them: characters and narrators whose consciousnesses are more available to us than those of others, to whom the function of seeing has to some extent been delegated.[28] They are vanishing points within the text; hovering, like the omniscient narrator, between omniscience and character, they express omniscience's contradictory need to be at once inside and outside character. Personalizing the impersonal and depersonalizing the personal, they conflate and confuse narratological and characterological functions. As narratorial surrogates, their immateriality enables them to act out a fantasy of omniscience even as their status as characters reveals its projective structure, the displacements that arise when a subject subjects others. And, as loci for reader identification, they situate the reader, much as a painting's vanishing point determines a spectator's perspective. Mirroring them, the reader also becomes a vanishing point: a reflection of what is defined by its unavailability to representation.[29]

---

28. See Gérard Genette, *Narrative Discourse* (Ithaca: Cornell University Press, 1980). For another discussion of focalization, see Rimmon-Kenan, *Narrative Fiction*, ch. 6.
29. Christian Metz locates the vanishing point at the back of the specta-

These semi-omnis̆cient figures disturb what are ordinarily taken to be the boundaries between first- and third-person narration, boundaries already disturbed by the nineteenth century's commonplace belief in physiognomy and phrenology. As one description of physiognomy has it, "the soul, pervading the human frame throughout, manifests itself in the face, hands, neck, ears, hair, voice, all parts and every habitual movement."[30] If everyone can be "read," individuals become vulnerable to one another's reading, and unseen observation—the ability to read others without being read oneself—becomes an almost inescapable fantasy of experiencing power over others. The same author writes that "the ability to read with unfailing accuracy the characters of his neighbours, to put his finger on their foibles, and in fact to lay bare their weaknesses . . . puts into [the physiognomist's] hands a lever of the most powerful character" (23). The transparency physiognomy attributes to individuals is thus a claim about the epistemological power invested in the reader's position, a power that inevitably shapes relations between individuals.

Indeed, omniscience is not a fantasy limited to third-person narrators, but one whose epistemological implications transcend particular narrative modes, breaking down distinctions between first and third person. Thus nineteenth-century first-person narrators, such as David Copperfield or Charlotte Brontë's Jane Eyre or Lucy Snowe, often perform the kind of reading usually ascribed only to omniscient narrators, collapsing the difference between the supposed limitations of first-person narration and the unlimitedness of third-person narration. They may "disappear" from their narratives in order to focus on others (hiding, as Jane Eyre does in the living room at Thornfield, in order to observe unseen) or may seem to disappear as a result of their focus on others. (And we might argue,

---

tor's head, where the film projector is, "precisely where phantasy locates the 'focus' of all vision." "All of us have experienced our own look," he writes," as a cone of light . . . whose vicariousness draws successive and variable slices of obscurity from nothingness wherever and whenever it comes to rest." *The Imaginary Signifier* (Bloomington: Indiana University Press, 1982), pp. 50–51.

30. Joseph Simms, introduction to *Physiognomy Illustrated* (New York: Murray Hill, 1891).

as I do about David Copperfield and Esther Summerson, that this is why they are narrators.) Of course, this type of reading is not the same as mind reading, though it often functions as such, as for instance when Rochester, dressed as a gypsy in order to keep Jane from seeing him, reads her face. But even if first-person narrators cannot read minds, as omniscient narrators can, other characters often prove to be quite legible to them—more legible, in fact, than they as narrators are to us. "I never thought anything about myself, distinctly" (170), writes David Copperfield, claiming elsewhere that he knows of Little Em'ly "what she had been unable to repress when her heart lay open to me by accident" (265). Similarly, Brontë's Lucy Snowe writes that John Graham "laid himself open to my observation."[31] For these narrators, face reading *is* mind reading—reading the body is reading the mind—though, rather than being invisible demons, these are actual bodies who, required to recount more than they might realistically observe, must find excuses for their presence. Thus, in order to read Mme. Beck's face, Lucy "followed her to the carriage, and looked in after she was seated and the door closed" (270).

The omniscient narrator is a further displacement of the personal, a more completely effaced observer. There are no "third persons," but only first persons wearing masks of invisibility. And the donning of such masks betrays an anxiety about being observed, as these first-person narrators make clear when, like Dickens's omniscient narrators, they make the act of observation their explicit concern. Lucy Snowe carefully keeps track of Mme. Beck's spying; David Copperfield keeps his eye on the eyes of those who watch him. Foregrounding the activity of watching, these narrators distance themselves from potential objectification, maintaining a position of vigilance, self-conscious about the activity of watching. But as in Sartre's famous keyhole scene—in which the spy gazing through the keyhole discovers that he is the object of another's gaze—by gazing on another, the narrator only imagines that

---

31. Charlotte Brontë, *Villette* (London: Penguin, 1979), p. 162. Subsequent page references are given in the text.

he escapes the other's gaze.[32] Watching the watchers, these personified narrators betray their own anxiety about being watched, attempting to neutralize or naturalize their own watching by directing attention away from themselves.

Given the way physiognomical reading in the nineteenth century threatened to render individuals transparent to one another, a fantasy of omniscience seems inevitable. And it is necessarily a fantasy in which individuals—"first persons"— participate. Positioning themselves in espistemologically superior positions with regard to other characters, first-person narrators often reveal a desire for superior knowledge and power similar to that which an omniscient narrator possesses in relation to characters. In both cases, this kind of reading brings to the surface of the text the fact that "narrator" and "character" signify positions of knowledge.

And yet what is the nature of the knowledge these narrators gain by reading the faces of others? Keeping themselves out of view, such first-person narrators indulge in what is intuitively recognizable as projective reading. As they watch others, they also reveal, to those who read them, their own concerns and desires. In order to articulate the projective tensions to which the omniscient gaze gives rise, I have made use of Lacanian ideas of mirroring and displacement. Lacan's mirror stage, in which subjectivity is formed via the individual's perception of his or her own image in the external world, provides a scenario for dramatizing the sense of self-division displayed by a number of Dickens's characters and narrators. At various moments in the novels, in an almost allegorical enactment of the mirror stage, the omniscient observer seems to be produced by the disruption of an imaginary identification with the mother.[33] In *The Old Curiosity Shop* and *David Copperfield*, for example, the effaced narrator emerges when the personified narrator fails to find himself represented in his

32. Jean-Paul Sartre, "The Look," in *Being and Nothingness*, pt. III: 4 (New York: Washington Square Press, 1966).

33. See Jacques Lacan, "The Mirror Stage," in *Ecrits: A Selection*, trans. Alan Sheridan (New York: Norton, 1977), pp. 1–7.

mother's eyes. But that failure is also a success, a displacement in which a character moves out of the realm of subjection to the gaze, avoiding the gazes of others by becoming the invisible narrator. As in Sartre's example, to be observed is to be transformed from subject to object. But to imagine oneself as bodiless, as invisible, is to occupy without threat the position of the observing other. These transformations between characters in Dickens's work reproduce the relationship between omniscient narrator and character, hinting at the presence, behind the mask of invisibility, of a subject who is aware of and anxious about the possibility of becoming an object for others.

As my use of Lacan suggests, the problematic of omniscience as I define it here intersects with contemporary theoretical accounts of the problematics of the gaze. In nineteenth-century British literature, the values projected by that gaze are most frequently those of the dominant social group—white, male, and middle class. Dickens's omniscient narrators are no exception to this general rule. The figures I have called "vanishing points" might be said to complicate the issue of gender, however; in *Bleak House* and *Dombey and Son*, for instance, an implicitly male omniscience is complemented and doubled by a female perspective located within the confines of the plot. In order to make its point, that is, a male consciousness— whether we imagine it as the personal consciousness of the author or the prevailing attitude of the culture—temporarily takes on what it imagines to be a female mode of vision. In such instances, what I have described as omniscience's characteristic tension between external and internal views becomes a gendered difference. And while Dickens's use of female narrators and characters gives us a strong sense of the difference gender makes to a discussion of narrative form and Victorian fiction, it also provides a clear example of the way "female" points of view can be appropriated by and employed to reinforce dominant cultural values.

I thus argue here that character is a metaphor for what omniscience projects outside itself, and that the limitations of vision or knowledge that define character in Dickens's work underscore the dominance (and hence invisibility) of the narrator's position, at the same time revealing the projective quality of the narrator's representations. My purpose is to provide sociological, historical, and epistemological content for categories that are, in traditional narrative theory, socially and historically empty by demonstrating the way in which a difference between the ownership of knowledge and the objects it constitutes is inscribed within and required by both Victorian culture and omniscience's fantasmatics of knowledge.

I have chosen works which allow for—and indeed inspired—the elaboration of the problematic of omniscience as I have outlined it here. Though I move from Boz to *Our Mutual Friend*, tracing the disappearance of the personified narrator, my approach is not fundamentally developmental. Dickens's work does move away from personified narration—Boz and Humphrey—toward the distant, invisible narrator of *Our Mutual Friend*, but since I view the second as a transformation and displacement of the first, I am more interested in suggesting similarities between personified and disembodied narrators than in arguing for a significant change from one kind of omniscience to another. And while each chapter touches on similar concerns—the construction of the narrator who desires to stand outside the self, the projective relationship between narrator and characters, the concern with watching and spying—each also focuses on issues suggested by the individual works.

I begin with Dickens's semi-omniscient narrator Boz and the problematic of narratorial sympathy in the *Sketches*, exploring the tension between commercialization and disinterest both in that text and in the sketches narrated by Dickens's later construction, the Uncommercial Traveller. Chapter 2 discusses the shift from personified to omniscient narration in *The Old Curiosity Shop*, positing "curiosity" as the novel's name for its subject/object confusion, while chapter 3 focuses on *Dombey and Son*'s construction of the family, private life, and "natural" feeling. In chapter 4 we see how *David Copperfield* and *Bleak House* allow for an articulation of the first-person narrator's participation in the omniscient fantasy and of the significance of gender for each narrative's form. And chapter 5 discusses the function of surprise in Dickens's omniscience.

In a manner that might be said to resemble omniscient narration, then, each chapter takes a somewhat different perspective on the book's general subject. It would however be contradictory, given my argument, to suggest that these approaches could be added together to yield a comprehensive view—or overview—of narrative omniscience or of Dickens. My hope instead is that what follows will provide readers with new angles on Victorian fiction, on Dickens, and on narrative, disrupting rather than satisfying a sense of readerly omniscience.

❨ 1 ❩

Boz and the Business of Narration

Dickens's narrative persona in the *Sketches* resembles his later conception for the "Shadow" behind *Household Words*, and the term "shadow" serves as a useful metaphor for both. That figure was intended to link the disparate topics with which the journal dealt, "to bind them all together" yet remain vague enough so that "any of the writers" might "maintain it without difficulty." Equipped, unlike Boz, with a personal history and family, the Shadow would also "loom as a fanciful thing all over London . . . a sort of semi-omniscient, omnipresent, intangible creature" (Forster, II: 419). As I have suggested, "semi-omniscience" describes the ambivalent form Dickens's narrators take. The narrator provides a focus for the readers' perceptions—we see "with" him—but remains invisible, moving among characters without becoming one himself. But the phrase also points to the tension this activity involves, for the observation of others puts the personified narrator in a dubious position. What is his purpose? What is his relation to those he observes, what the nature of his curiosity about them? What, indeed, is semi-omniscience? The narrator who is also a character cannot be omniscient, since he is a part of the scene he observes. Yet by positioning himself as observer he asserts his distance and difference from those he describes.

If we consider Roland Barthes's formulation that character may be located at the convergence of semes which fasten onto a name, whereupon "the name becomes a subject," we might consider the difficulty of accumulating semes to link with the name "Boz," and, furthermore, the deliberate playfulness and unreality of the name itself, which calls attention to its fictionality.[1] While we can attribute various attitudes to the narrator, we have little in the way of personal reflections to establish a character "Boz" whose particularities and idiosyncrasies are commensurate with those of the characters he describes. Idiosyncrasy, in fact, is precisely what Boz avoids, purchasing his freedom precisely *at the expense of* character, of identity insofar as the *Sketches* define it. "Boz" points away from the identity of author and narrator toward that of character; "character" appears as something the narrator locates elsewhere, something he can perceive clearly because he does not inhabit it. Thus even as the narrator's use of the third-person plural makes a gesture toward inclusion, inviting identification, it also marks the speaker's perspective as distinct and superior.[2]

The *Sketches* are subtitled "Illustrative of Every-Day Life and Every-Day People." Rendering the "every-day," however, the narrator inevitably separates himself from it, inhabiting, as he does, the perceptual space from which to see it. The sketch form itself, as Richard Stein points out, suggests both a lack of attention and a superiority to its subject matter. It displays the narrator's mobility as he passes from subject to subject, creating a sense of fragmentation which conveys not the narrator's concession to the overwhelming scope of his task, but rather his ability to rise above it.[3] And that sense of mobility is heightened by the constraints that define the lives of many of the *Sketches'* characters. Where they are fixed in character and routine, Boz is mobile; where they are limited by social and economic circumstances, the narrator seems to have risen above such circumstances.

The *Sketches* articulate an incommensurability of subject and object which recurs throughout Dickens's work. Boz establishes his narrative position by seeing what characters fail

1. Barthes, *S/Z*, pp. 190–91.
2. Angus Easson touches on these points in "Who is Boz? Dickens and his Sketches," *Dickensian* 81 (1985): 13–21, though he claims that Boz's use of the third person plural reinforces his "kinship" with his subject.
3. Richard Stein writes that the word "sketch . . . connotes effortlessness, and thus the work of a genteel amateur . . . the observer can remain interested but detached because of a portraiture that does not pass beyond certain limits of scope and specificity." See *Victoria's Year: English Literature and Culture, 1837–1838* (New York: Oxford University Press, 1987), p. 27.

to see, which includes not only, in the descriptive sketches, the city of London, but, in the stories, the inevitable failure of many characters' projects, particularly those involving social ambition. Organization and identity are external matters; characters are caught within structures they cannot perceive from the outside. And character is both a metaphor for such structures and the primary means by which they are articulated. Boz's knowledge thus reveals itself to be dependent upon the construction of a particularly constrained fictional universe. Just as, in G. K. Chesterton's image, Dickensian coziness is grounded in the discomfort surrounding it, so too is the narrator's omniscience founded on the opposition between characterological limitation and narratological knowledge.[4] In order to be omniscient, the narrator must have something to be omniscient about; he must define himself in opposition to those more limited than himself. In effect, he must create limited subjects. The *Sketches* afford us an early look at the production of the Dickensian subject and of a narrative presence whose business is to evade, and avoid, subjection.

The narratological and epistemological difference between subject and object in the *Sketches* is also a social one. Indeed, as Boz articulates them, these categories are indistinguishable from one another. As many readers have pointed out, Boz is a *flâneur*, a connoisseur of street life, and the *flâneur* is an ambivalent figure, one whose "paradoxical street activity" lies between "the purposive and the non-purposive."[5] In order to observe, writes Walter Benjamin, the *flâneur* must be in his primary place, the street, and yet he is inherently out of place there. "Let the many attend to their daily affairs . . . the man of leisure can indulge in the perambulations only if as such he is already out of place." Drawn to the crowd only to turn his back on it, he "becomes deeply involved with them, only to relegate them to oblivion with a single glance of contempt."[6]

4. G. K. Chesterton, *Charles Dickens* (New York: Schocken, 1965), p. 164.
5. Michael Hollington, "Dickens the Flâneur," *Dickensian* 77 (1981): 78.
6. Walter Benjamin, "On Some Motifs in Baudelaire," in *Illuminations*, ed. Hannah Arendt (New York: Schocken, 1969), p. 172.

The difference between "purposive" and "non-purposive" activity is suggestive, for the sketch narrator's purpose lies in his apparent non-purposiveness. What is an unavoidable fact of daily life for others—participation in public life in the city—is the focus of his interest. Lewis Mumford has argued that the urban aggregation characteristic of nineteenth-century cities was, in part, typified by "the atomic individual," a figure for whom "to guard his property, to protect his rights, to ensure his freedom of choice and freedom of enterprise, was the whole duty of government."[7] In what Mumford calls the "new capitalist city," each individual's primary concern is the development of his own interest, each "enterprising man" is in fact a kind of despot, presiding over his own little kingdom— an idea that Mumford refers to as "the myth of the untrammeled individual." But as the *Sketches* make abundantly clear, none are more trammeled than these "men of habit" who trudge, heads bowed, to and from their city offices each morning, their freedom—if such is their fantasy—in abeyance. It is Boz, rather, who enacts the fantasy of the untrammeled individual for his readers, finding interest in what the man on his way to business cannot take the time to see. He is the man whose business is his pleasure—one who finds his capital in what must be, for others, incidental: in the interstices of their lives.

As he turns the seemingly inconsequential material of daily life into capital, then, the sketch narrator's business absorbs what business itself has left out of its domain. In fact, by the time of—and in the figure of—the Uncommercial Traveller, Dickens has thoroughly thematized the way in which literary sketching makes what appears to be idleness issue into labor.[8] If nothing escapes Boz's or the Uncommercial's eye, it is be-

7. Lewis Mumford, *The Culture of Cities* (New York: Harcourt Brace Jovanovich, 1970), p. 145.

8. While critics tend to emphasize the difference between Boz and the Uncommercial, I see the latter figure as a more explicit version of the former one, displaying the same tendency to turn human interest into business. For another perspective, see Rosalind Vallance, "From Boz to the Uncommercial," *Dickensian* 63 (1966): 27–33.

cause everything can be turned to account. In making use of material the man of business ignores, Dickens's sketch narrators thus prove their business ability. And what remains implicit in the *Sketches* becomes, in the later work, the narrator's persona: "Figuratively speaking, I travel for the great firm of Human Interest Brothers, and have rather a large connection in the fancy goods way. Literally speaking, I am always wandering here and there . . . seeing many little things, which, because they interest me, I think may interest others" (*UT*, 1–2).

As an "amateur observer," whose livelihood depends on not seeing in a habitual way, the Uncommercial is an apt figure for the sketch narrator. The idea of "uncommercial travelling" is wonderfully disingenuous, for, while not selling *to* those he encounters in the course of his travels, the narrator's intent is rather to sell what he can make of his interest in them—to sell *them*. Uncommercial traveling provides the justification lacking in the *Sketches*, but it is a strained one, suggesting by negation what is in fact truly the case: that uncommercial traveling is indeed commercial. "Business" is a pretense that enables observation, a pretense that Dickens himself used. ("In 1867, he told an interviewer that while walking he often resorted to disguise, or would act like a rent collector, or other person on business, to avoid attracting notice."[9]) Both the "human interest" passage and the Uncommercial's persona may be said to register an awareness of the inherently ambivalent nature of the project of making money by putting human interest into circulation. At the same time, the project represents an attempt to overcome that ambivalence.

Boz and the Uncommercial comment in various ways on their own apparent idleness, which contrasts so sharply with the street life that provides their subject, and both collections register the omnipresence of business in Mumford's new capitalist city. Indeed, the tension between the busy and the idle sometimes becomes the narrator's explicit focus. Both narra-

9. F. S. Schwarzbach, *Dickens and the City* (London: Athlone Press, 1979), p. 236.

tors are fascinated by places where business is conducted at times when it usually is not (what the Uncommercial calls "the hushed resorts of business"). In "Making a Night of It," idleness is reckoned in business terms. "Making a night of it" means "the borrowing of several hours from tomorrow morning and adding them to the night before, and manufacturing a compound night of the whole" (267). And as a last touch, "London Recreations" glances at the waiters who, having supplied "Sunday-pleasurers" with tea, "count their glasses and their gains" (96).

Making their own curiosity an explicit concern, Boz and the Uncommercial comment on the way in which their observation seems unconnected to any business, and therefore, even to them, strange. In the absence of any other motivation, Boz cites "curiosity." "We felt an irrepressible curiosity to witness this interview, although it is hard to tell why," he writes of witnessing a young woman's meeting with her assailant in "The Hospital Patient" (241). "Actuated, we hope, by a higher feeling than mere curiosity," he attempts to befriend a woman and her dying son in order to hear their story (45). He observes as if compelled—"We could not help stopping and observing them" (197)—even though compulsion is the term he usually reserves for the behavior of others. (The "man of habit" in the sketch "Thoughts About People" "walks up and down . . . not as if he were doing it for pleasure and recreation, but as if it were a matter of compulsion" [216].) And the Uncommercial, whose very title captures the ambivalence of business that does not appear to be business, similarly foregrounds his "idle employment" (*UT*, 309). The status of the non-participant observer is repeatedly questioned, the ambiguity of his position brought to the fore. But that ambiguity, while pointing to the true unease of making human interest into business, also serves a purpose. As the narrator displays his desire to sympathize, he registers his epistemological and social difference from his ostensible objects of sympathy.

Both collections of sketches thematize the difference between the narrator's perceptions and those of others, a difference which depends upon the difference between his business and theirs. In such sketches as "The Streets—Morning" or "The Streets—Night" the sketch narrator is situated where he would not be were he a costermonger, a servant, or a man of business on his way to the office. His typical strategy is to define and describe what he sees to an imagined, "bewildered" observer, who can't make sense of what he sees, or to a habitual city-dweller, who—according to Boz—doesn't see at all. The sketch then proceeds to point out the difference between that observer's perception and the narrator's. Boz sees what goes unseen by those who "brush quickly by you, steadily plodding on to business" (59), "mere passive creatures of habit and endurance" (215), and what is for the imagined stranger "a maze of streets, courts, lanes, and alleys" (69) is ordered by the narrator's perception. In "Seven Dials," "[T]he peculiar character of these streets, and the close resemblance each one bears to his neighbour, by no means tends to decrease the bewilderment in which the unexperienced wayfarer through 'the Dials' finds himself involved" (71). At the mercy of his surroundings, the observer "stands Belzoni-like, at the entrance of seven obscure passages, uncertain which to take" (69). Boz asserts coherence in opposition to the idea of incoherence, illegibility, or simply the failure or inability to pay attention, as exemplified by an observer created for the purpose of this opposition: one who avoids seeing, has no time to look, or perceives only a confused and fragmentary reality.

But Boz himself encompasses his subject by breaking it up into fragments—manageable pieces—as well as by using "types" representative of what he calls "classes." "Our parish" stands for any parish; the "man of habit" is merely "one of this class" (214). Telescoping the city and its inhabitants, the narrator effectively contains the city's multiplicity by shrinking or reducing it. The contrast between the narrator's freedom and his subjects' constraint thus depends in part upon Boz's characters being themselves marked, shrunken in spirit and size, as many of their names—"Tibbs," "Tuggs," "Minns," "Watkins Tottle"—suggest. Appropriately, the sketch that opens the collection, "Our Parish," alludes to this encapsulating technique: "How much is contained in those two short

words—'The Parish!'" (1). "How much" is contained, or
would be contained, by the narrator himself.

Particularity is sacrificed to an idea of order which flattens
out differences. Thus in "Seven Dials," "Every room has its
separate tenant, and every tenant is, by the same mysterious
dispensation which causes a country curate to 'increase and
multiply' most marvellously, generally the head of a numerous
family" (72). "The man in the shop, perhaps, is in the baked
'jemmy' line, or the fire-wood and hearth-stone line. . . . Then
there is an Irish labourer and *his* family in the back kitchen, and
a jobbing man—carpet-beater and so forth—with *his* family in
the front one" (72). These accounts are finally as structured by
the habitual as the perceptions of those men of habit Boz
rejects. The narrator need not see because he already knows—
as, he presumes, do his readers ("and so forth"). Order turns
out to mean sameness and repetition; the narrator's rhetoric
betrays his distance from those he would describe. Boz "sees"
only what he can easily contain, and his descriptions bear the
signs of that containment.

Classifications regularize what might otherwise seem an
incomprehensible multiplicity of individuals: the individual is
replaced by the group and the group replaces the individual.
The principle of the "Character" sketches is accordingly one of
likeness. Mr. John Dounce is one of a class of "old boys";
"shabby-genteel people" are represented by one shabby-
genteel man (262); Mr. Bung in "The Broker's Man" is "one
of the careless, good-for-nothing, happy fellows, who float,
cork-like, on the surface, for the world to play at hockey with"
(25). "A numerous race are these red-faced men. . . . So, just
to hold a pattern up to know the others by, we took his
likeness at once, and put him in here" (239). "If we had to
make a classification of society, there are a particular kind of
men who we should immediately set down under the head of
'Old Boys'" (244).

Characters are further identified by their repetitive, com-
pulsive behavior, which Boz sometimes recounts in the present tense (as in the first quotation) to suggest its habitual
nature.

The old lady sees scarcely any company, except the little girls before noticed, each of whom has always a regular fixed day for a periodical tea-drinking with her. . . . Her name always heads the list of any benevolent subscriptions. . . . Her entrance into church on Sundays is always the signal for a little bustle in the side aisle. . . . Thus, with the annual variation of a trip to some quiet place on the sea-coast, passes the old lady's life. (10–11)

They always sat, in the same places, doing precisely the same things at the same hour. The eldest Miss Willis used to knit, the second to draw, the two others to play duet on the piano. They seemed to have no separate existence, but to have made up their minds to winter through life together.

There was something in the man's manner and appearance which told us, we fancied, his whole life, or rather his whole day, for a man of this sort has no variety of days. (216)

The idea of the habitual makes it possible to represent an entire life in sketch form since one day is the same as every other. Yet it seems to be the case in the *Sketches* not only that particular characters are creatures of habit, but that character itself depends upon the idea of repetition. Indeed, character in the *Sketches* is a reductive version of what is generally considered constitutive of character in the traditional novel. "The main principles of cohesion . . . are repetition, similarity, contrast, and implication . . . the repetition of the same character trait 'invites' labelling it as a character-trait."[10] And, relying as they do on the idea of sameness and duplication, the stories and descriptive sketches reveal a disturbing subtext in which individual identity dissolves in a mélange of likenesses. Characters are frequently described as copies of one another. Miss Charlotte Tuggs is "fast ripening" into an image of her mother (335); Miss Malderton "looked like her daughter multiplied by two" (357); the Misses Crumpton dress "like twins" (323); and the four Miss Willises throw the neighborhood into consternation by announcing that "*We* are going to marry Mr. Robinson" (15). Two or more turnkeys "look like multiplications of the first one" (197). Rather than simply being referred to oth-

10. Rimmon-Kenan, *Narrative Fiction*, p. 39.

ers for the purpose of elaborating a description, these characters are already likenesses, copies of one another.

The idea of likeness filters into Boz's language in terms which suggest both the encapsulation the sketch form tries to achieve and the individuality it necessarily leaves out in doing so. The brevity of the *Sketches* seems to acknowledge the hurriedness of city life, which requires a contracted account and the use of a language of repetition. "Mr. Thomas Potter . . . was a clerk in the city, and Mr. Robert Smithers was a ditto in the same" (266). "The Miss Maldertons were dressed in skyblue satin trimmed with artificial flowers; and Mrs. M. . . . in ditto ditto" (357). Again, Boz relies on the reader—the habitual reader—to fill in the blanks, encapsulating what has already been said or what the reader may be expected to know.

The *Sketches'* emphasis on similarity and repetition is balanced by their interest in the peculiar. Even the most ordinary characters seem pathological in their ordinariness, as if ordinariness were a disease the narrator is fortunate to have escaped. When Boz announces that, given only six "parochial sketches," he will select for character description "the most peculiar" (13), he points toward a principle of selection that has, oddly, received less attention than the idea that the *Sketches* are "realistic."[11] Yet the peculiar and the ordinary, or typical, are not so far apart. The type is, after all, a kind of caricature, a fiction supposed to represent the lowest common denominator. And, as in the following description of London apprentices, the typical and the peculiar can merge: "Each of the gentlemen carried a thick stick, with a large tassel at the top, which he occasionally twirled gracefully round; and the whole four, by way of looking easy and unconcerned, were walking with a paralytic swagger irresistibly ludicrous" (219). The four become one in description: distinguished by the

11. For example, Gissing writes: "Veracity I take to be the high merit of these sketches" (*Charles Dickens: A Critical Study* [New York: Dodd, Mead & Co., 1924], p. 43). On the other hand, for Michael Hollington, "there is no question, in these early works, of 'realistic' character portrayal": *Dickens and the Grotesque* (London and Sydney: Croom Helm, 1984), p. 40. See this work for a discussion of Dickens's "peculiar" characters.

details of their clothing and their "ludicrous" manner, they are a single body, a group become an individual.

Georg Simmel writes that the city gives rise to an emphasis on difference and a tendency toward eccentricity as a necessary means of expressing individuality.

> There is the difficulty of giving one's own personality a certain status within the framework of metropolitan life. . . . This leads ultimately to the strangest eccentricities, to specifically metropolitan extravagances of self-distanciation, of caprice, of fastidiousness, the meaning of which is no longer to be found in the content of such activity itself but rather in its being a form of "being different"—of making oneself noticeable.[12]

Yet such efforts can result in a uniformity of eccentricity. A form of "being different" is, after all, a form, and even while attempting to differentiate themselves from one another, individuals may resemble one another in their common attempts at difference. In the *Sketches*, distinct as individual characters may be, they are alike in the form their difference from the narrator takes.

But the tension between the typical and the peculiar, or the general and the idiosyncratic—the two poles by which character in the *Sketches* is articulated—might also be understood by asking what Dickens's narrator and readers could have at stake in such representations. While Boz's vagueness as a character seems to open up a space for readerly identification, his goal—the illustration of "every-day" life—implicitly makes his readers the objects of his observation. The idiosyncratic comes to stand for and signify character, that which narrator and readers may define themselves against. But, as we have seen, the narrator also defines himself in opposition to the ordinary, the common, the habitual. While the typical may allow readers to see themselves reflected in what they read (Boz's allusions to what readers presumably already know certainly do so), both the typical and the idiosyncratic also leave room for readers to inhabit a space outside charac-

---

12. Georg Simmel, *On Individuality and Social Forms*, ed. Donald N. Levine (Chicago: University of Chicago Press, 1971), p. 336.

ter, since what is represented is always defined by its difference from the perceiver. The term "peculiar" means characteristic as well as strange, and Boz's mode of representation
allows readers to define the peculiar and the ordinary as familiar and yet as other.

Boz's voyeurism is frequently directed toward those lower
on the social scale than himself. In an early preface to the
Sketches, Dickens compares the book to an ascending balloon
which bears aloft "not only himself, but all his hopes of future
fame, and all his chances of future success."[13] This image of
soaring ambition contrasts strikingly with the frequent depiction, within the *Sketches*, of downward movement. Boz is
pervasively concerned with the representation of poverty and
distress and, in particular, with the process of decline—in
London, London's shops, and London's inhabitants. He often
speaks from the perspective of an unspecified earlier time, a
bygone era of gentility, in comparison with which the present
represents a falling away, thereby distinguishing his perspective temporally from that of his characters, who live in, and
thus cannot really see, the world they inhabit. In "Scotland
Yard," change equals loss: "how have its old customs changed;
and how has the ancient simplicity of its inhabitants faded
away!" (67). "The First of May" tells, from the perspective of
"our young days," about the "decay" of May-Day; a hackney-
coach is "a remnant of past gentility" (85). And "The Parish"
traces the decline of the Pauper Schoolmaster, whom "it would
be difficult" for his former acquaintances to recognize (6).

Boz's interest in the shabby-genteel, or in brokers' shops,
resembles fascination rather than sympathy. He is amused
and excited, as if decay and decline were mere abstractions,
far from possessing any human significance. In "Shops and
Their Tenants," he is intrigued by signs of deterioration in one
shop after another. "We were somewhat curious to ascertain
what would be the next stage—for that the place had no
chance of surviving, was perfectly clear. . . . We were in a

13. Quoted by Ellen Moers in *The Dandy* (London: Secker and Warburg,
1960), p. 219.

fever of expectation: we exhausted conjecture" (62). The world Boz represents is governed by a relentless pull downward, even though the details of individual stories easily go without saying: "A prison, and the sentence—banishment or the gallows. . . . We had no clue to the end of the tale; but it was easy to guess its termination" (78). His interest in decline is an extension of his general interest in the downtrodden, the representation of which seems intended to arouse sympathy in his readers. But the idea of sympathy conflicts with the narrator's evident difference and distance from those he observes. The desire to look is at odds with anxiety about what is being looked at.[14]

One of the *Sketches'* critics has argued that the collection includes essentially two kinds of narratives: descriptive sketches, the purpose of which is to elicit the readers' sympathy, and satiric stories, usually concerned with a failed attempt at social advancement. Virgil Grillo makes the case that these two kinds of sketches should be ascribed to two distinctly different narrators: a sympathetic sketch narrator, and an ironic story narrator.[15] But while such a division proves useful for discussing the attributes of each, it obscures the sense in which sympathy and irony are the two contradictory poles of omniscience, representing the desire to participate—to see from the inside—as well as to remain unconstrained by circumstances and hence outside character. It also obscures the fact that Dickens used only a single narrator, attempting to join these contradictory impulses in and by means of a single consciousness. But the impulses behind sympathy and irony are finally not so different from one another. By positing a specific individual or group as a subject for investigation, both promote a sense of estrangement from the other being investi-

14. According to J. Hillis Miller, the deterministic vision of the *Sketches* is directly related to their metonymic method. See "The Fiction of Realism: *Sketches by Boz, Oliver Twist*, and Cruikshank's Illustrations," in Ada Nisbet and Blake Nevius, eds., *Dickens Centennial Essays* (Berkeley and Los Angeles: University of California Press, 1971), pp. 101–2.

15. Virgil Grillo, *Charles Dickens's "Sketches by Boz": End in the Beginning* (Boulder: Colorado Associated University Press, 1974).

gated. Though sympathy supposedly transcends difference, it in fact depends on establishing the difference it proposes to transcend. And comedy, as René Girard writes, depends on an underlying anxiety about similarity.

> The man who laughs is just about to be enveloped into the pattern of which his victim is already a part; as he laughs he both welcomes and rejects the perception of the structure into which the object of his laughter is already caught; he welcomes it insofar as it is someone else who is caught in it and he tries to keep it away from himself. . . . As an assertion of superiority, in the more intellectual forms of the comic, laughter really means a denial of reciprocity.[16]

In fact, the ironic stories and the sympathetic sketches are more closely related than Grillo thinks. On the one hand, the sketches promote the idea of sympathy for the poor and downtrodden; on the other, the stories, by satirizing attempts at social mobility, implicitly argue for the fixedness and distinctness of social classes. The impulse behind the sympathetic sketches seems to be a fear of falling which has as its counterpart the stories' anxiety about social mobility. Both the sympathetic sketches and the satiric stories provide ways to entertain and contain potentially threatening material, and the tension between sympathy and irony leaves an undefined middle space—what we might call an undefined middle-class space—which the narrator implicitly inhabits. As the stories tacitly warn against attempting to rise in society and the sketches depict the dangers of the social fall, the mobile narrator insists upon his subjects' immobility.

Boz's own mobility depends on rigidly fixed boundaries which allow for no uncertainty or transgression on the part of those who inhabit them. The tales are largely warnings against transgression, accounts of characters whose attempts to break out of rigidly patterned, habitual lives inevitably fail, returning them to situations the same or worse than

---

16. René Girard, "Perilous Balance: A Comic Hypothesis," in *"To Double Business Bound": Essays on Literature, Mimesis, Anthropology* (Baltimore: Johns Hopkins University Press, 1978), pp. 127–28.

before. The stories regularly tell of an individual, such as John Dounce, whose life takes a form something like the following:

> Regular as clockwork—breakfast at nine—dress and tittivate a little—down to the Sir Somebody's Head—a glass of ale and the paper—come back again, and take daughters out for a walk—dinner at three—glass of grog and a pipe—nap—tea—little walk—Sir Somebody's Head again—capital house—delightful evenings. (245)

The insignificance of Dounce's activities is relayed by the encapsulated, telegraphic description; the terms "capital" and "delightful" have an edge to them, suggesting the littleness of Dounce's aspirations. The story tells of only a small desire— Dounce falls in love with the oyster woman—but even that ambition, which disrupts Dounce's normal routine, proves too great for Boz. The lady refuses him, Dounce "rendered himself ridiculous to everybody," and the story ends up being "a warning to all uxorious old boys" (249). This type of warning against ambition is characteristic of the *Sketches*. Horatio Sparkins pretends to be "above" his business (365); the mistake of "The Mistaken Milliner" is that she forgets to live "on her business and not above it" (250). Mr. Augustus Cooper, similarly, ends by "losing his ambition for society" (261) after that ambition leads to embarrassment and failure. Tuggs, in "The Tuggses at Ramsgate," is a grocer, Sparkins an assistant at a cheap shop: their stories also tell of the failure of their social ambitions.

Thus, even though the stories are generally considered attacks on hypocrisy and pretension, one can easily perceive in them a concern with and anxiety about social mobility. Characters inevitably give their "true" class away. "The Mistaken Milliner" is mistaken to think she can "come out" in society, and her inability to sing sends her back in again. Horatio Sparkins, through a series of mishaps, reveals himself to be not a young gentleman "about to be called," but "the junior partner in a slippery firm of some three weeks' existence" (369). These stories are all lessons in not living "above one's business." In them, social position is inscribed in, and fixed *as*, character. Boz's characters simply cannot escape the social positions in which he finds them. But the transgression Boz refuses his characters he nevertheless enacts in his sketching. Depicting the "every-day" for those middle-class readers who might not see it with their own eyes, Boz provides a justification for his own transgression of social boundaries. And his interest in social ambition reveals his anxiety about it, telling us that those "others" he sketches represent a possible future for himself.

The "sympathetic" sketches deal not so much with attempts to rise socially as with what Boz presents as an inevitable process of decline. And what attracts him is not so much the opportunity to sympathize as the public nature of decline itself. Boz is fascinated less by the shabby-genteel man as sympathetic object, for instance, than by shabby-gentility as a public exhibition of decline. These sketches emphasize their subjects' awareness of, and shame about, falling from middle-class respectability, and the narrator's invisibility reinforces his imputations that decline—whether it takes place in the street or behind the closed door of the pawnbroker's shop—is always a public process.

Shabby-gentility is by definition public, since it refers to the way clothing reflects economic and social conditions. It identifies clothing, condition, and person: "[H]e grew more and more shabby-genteel every day. . . . At length, one of the buttons on the back of his coat fell off, and then the man himself disappeared, and we thought he was dead" (264). The shabby-genteel man "is" his clothing. "The truth flashed suddenly upon us: they [his clothes] had been 'revived.' It is a deceitful liquid that black and blue reviver; we have watched its effects on many a shabby-genteel man" (264). And Boz's attribution of shame to the shabby-genteel man—his publicizing not just the man's condition, but his shame about it—makes that awareness a central part of this sketch's appeal to their readers. What makes the shabby-genteel man pitiable is that he "feels his poverty and vainly strives to conceal it" (265). Significantly, he is afflicted not just by poverty, but by "conscious poverty" (263). His attempts at concealment, of course, only increase Boz's interest in him. Following his subjects into places in which they wish to remain unobserved, such as the pawnbroker's shop, the narrator presents decline as both shameful and impossible to hide. Further, the technique emphasizes the internalization of social shame. Even while the narrator must be present in order to describe, what he essentially describes is his own superfluity. Observed or not, the shabby-genteel man will feel and display his shame.

"The Pawnbroker's Shop" depicts four women in varying stages of decline: a woman and her daughter, relative newcomers to the shop; a gaudily dressed woman; and a fourth described as "the lowest of the low; dirty, unbonneted, flaunting, and slovenly." These figures exist only as illustrations of decline. Thus the gaudily dressed woman's daub of rouge "only serves as an index to the ravages of squandered health never to be regained, and lost happiness never to be restored" (194). She observes the mother and daughter:

> There is something in the glimpse she has just caught of her young neighbour, and in the sight of the little trinkets she has offered in pawn, that seems to have awakened in this woman's mind some slumbering recollection. . . . Her first hasty impulse was to bend forward as if to scan more minutely the appearance of her half-concealed companions; her next, on seeing them involuntarily shrink from her, to retreat to the back of the box, cover her face with her hands, and burst into tears.
> (194)

The slovenly woman also watches the pair. "Her curiosity was first attracted by the little she could see of the group; then her attention. The half-intoxicated leer changed to an expression of something like interest, and a feeling similar to that we have described, appeared for a moment, and only a moment, to extend itself even to her bosom" (194–95).

The "feeling similar to that we have described" is presumably sympathy (the running title in the Oxford edition, added by the editors, is "Feelings of Sympathy"), though no feeling has actually been described. And yet while seeming to invite sympathy, the sketch in fact displaces it, making sympathy its object and representing it in a series of actions: bending forward, becoming self-conscious and retreating, bursting into tears. Feeling is what the narrator regards rather than what he expresses or, rather, what he might seem to express—to sympathize with—simply because he represents it. The actions represented further suggest that sympathy is the same as, and emerges from, a recognition of self in another. What the two observing women seem to see in the daughter—particularly in her trinkets—is a representation of their past selves. For the daughter, similarly, the two women represent a possible future. And this is precisely Boz's point: "Who shall say," he writes, "how soon these women may change places? The last has but two more stages—the hospital and the grave. How many females situated as her two companions are, and as she may have been once, have terminated in the same wretched course" (195). The purpose of the sketch, writes Boz at its beginning, is the drawing of distinctions—"distinctions must be observed even in poverty"—but the function of these distinctions is the imagined collapse of these disparate figures, and innumerable others like them, into one (188).

The mother and daughter are oblivious both to their observation by the other women and to the shame which, the narrator tells us, invariably accompanies respectable individuals' visits to the pawnbroker's shop. The hardness of their lives, we are told, has "obliterated" in them the consciousness of "self-humiliation." As a result of watching the mother and daughter, however, the other women do display such humiliation. In fact, what the discovery of the past self signifies here—what sympathy turns out to be—is the recognition of the self *as* a figure of decline. What each woman sees in the other is her own shame, which manifests itself visibly and must be hidden, even though there is no one present to see it. It is, precisely, self-humiliation. The shop itself, with its booths hiding the more respectable clients from one another but remaining open to the reader's view, resembles, as Cruikshank's illustration suggests, Bentham's Panopticon. Shame, substituting for the booths, keeps these women isolated from one another even as they reveal their feelings to the reader.

These women make sympathy visible; they register it in their bodies. The narrator, having no body with which to display such feeling, watches them watch. By doing so, and by describing their responses, he provides an image of what

he cannot show in himself: what it would be like truly to
sympathize with, because one truly resembled, the objects of
one's contemplation. Using these women as mediators for his
observational activity—indeed, bestowing on them the terms
("attention," "curiosity," "interest") he uses elsewhere to describe his own activity—the narrator suggests the untoward-
ness of his very presence in the pawnbroker's shop, his violation of the privacy those who go there seek. His invisibility
signifies his safety, but also his anxiety. Like Perseus viewing

the Medusa's reflection in his shield, the narrator deflects any potential reciprocity between himself and his objects, keeping himself outside any exchange of identities. While presumably inviting sympathy, then, the sketch also indicates the hazards of sympathy, defined here as what one feels if one is already like, or in danger of becoming like, what one observes.

But the reader is invited to sympathize—not exactly with these women, but with their sympathy. Sympathy is what is not fallen about them: it is the lingering sign of humanity that appears "for a moment, and only for a moment" to extend itself "even" to the bosom of the woman called "the lowest of the low." "There are strange chords in the human heart," the sketch reads, "which will lie dormant through years of depravity and wickedness, but which will vibrate at last to some slight circumstance . . . connected by some undefined and indistinct association with past days that can never be recalled, and with bitter recollections from which even the most degraded creature in existence can never escape" (194). Situating and defining these women, the sketch also situates and defines its readers, for these women are both subjects and objects for readers. On the one hand, as subjects they provide a model: sympathy is presented as a sign of humanity, and readers are encouraged to find that humanity within themselves. On the other hand, sympathy is provoked by similarity, by the recognition of the self in the other: the women's sympathy is the same as their shame. The figure deserving of sympathy is thus she who recognizes herself as having fallen away from middle-class respectability. That consciousness registers, for the reader, the inscription of social position within the self as a constituent of character, affirming at the same time the middle-class reader's values, values from which these women have fallen and for which they evidently long. Inscribing social position, and self-consciousness about social position, as integral, internal aspects of self, the sketch displays for the reader a shame which seems natural: something readers might imagine recognizing in themselves and potentially revealing, even if no one is present to watch.

The progression from "curiosity" to "interest" to "sympathy" characterizes Boz's narrative strategy throughout the *Sketches*, differentiating him from the man of habit, whose face looks "as if it were incapable of bearing the expression of curiosity or interest" (215). Attention—"notice"—should lead to sympathy: "It is strange with how little notice, good, bad, or indifferent, a man may live and die in London. He awakens no sympathy in the breast of any single person; his existence is a matter of interest to no one save himself" (215). And much of what Boz notices is the presence or absence of sympathy in others:

> Curiosity has occasionally led us into both Courts at the Old Bailey. Nothing is so likely to strike the person who enters them for the first time, as the calm indifference with which the proceedings are conducted; every trial seems a mere matter of business. There is a great deal of form, but no compassion; considerable interest, but no sympathy. (198)

What catches the narrator's attention gradually leads him into speculation; the logical end of the process, it seems, should be sympathetic identification. But as "The Pawnbroker's Shop" demonstrates, the *Sketches* typically stop short of that final step, allowing the narrator room to differentiate himself from the objects of his description. Accordingly, what seems offered as sympathy often amounts to pointing out the absence of sympathy in others or representing sympathy in others. Individual sympathy is encouraged but also evaded. This problematization of sympathy may be said to reflect the transformation of sympathy into business so characteristic of charitable movements, reform societies, and governmental institutions in the nineteenth century. Where the eighteenth century imagines and repeatedly represents charity as the product of a face-to-face encounter between an observer and a figure in distress, the nineteenth century marks a transition to charity as an impersonal, administrative process, one which groups individual sufferers into classes and treats multiple bodies as one. Indeed, Boz and the Uncommercial often seek out their objects of sympathy in institutions—hospitals, prisons, courtrooms. Where the benevolent gentleman of an earlier age offered sympathy and coin, the sketch narrator simply reports. Seeking out in order to sympathize, he provides a model for a sympathy that intervenes, if at all, only from a distance.

In fact, Boz's ambivalence about his observational activity may express a tension between two cultural models of the middle-class subject's relationship to the poor. In Dickens's *Sketches*, that is, we might say that eighteenth-century benevolence encounters both nineteenth-century anxiety about social mobility and a nineteenth-century perception of the poor as requiring governmental scrutiny and regulation.[17] For it should be clear by now that those "others" Boz seeks out and describes—who wish to remain unseen or lie invisible behind the walls of prisons or hospitals—are not merely, or even primarily, objects of sympathy. Rather, they are figures of "interest" and "curiosity": "What London pedestrian is there who has not, at some time or other, cast a hurried glance through the wicket at which prisoners are admitted into this gloomy mansion, and surveyed the few objects he could discern, with an indescribable feeling of curiosity?" (196). At stake in that "hurried glance" is a displacement of sympathy by curiosity and interest—a displacement traceable, at least in part, to the institutionalization and bureaucratization of the poor discussed above. But the wall between observer and observed signifies not just the institution, but also the barrier erected and transgressed by the nineteenth-century middle-class observer, whose gaze inevitably wanders in the direction of what it defines as other to itself. The "indescribable" feeling one might have, walking past Newgate, thus remains undescribed; "curiosity" fills the place of that unspecified feeling. And yet curiosity situates its owner as much as it does those toward whom his gaze is directed.

17. Interestingly, in the *Sketches* the wandering that in earlier literature characterized both observer and suffering object—Wordsworth's narrators and vagrants, for instance—generally belongs to the observer alone, signifying his freedom.

❨ 2 ❩

Omniscience and Curiosity in
The Old Curiosity Shop

When, in "The Function of Criticism at the Present Time,"
Matthew Arnold chides the English for what he sees as a national preoccupation with the practical—the abrupt transposi-
tion of ideas "into the world of politics and practice"—he cites
for support the moral taint they attach to the word "curiosity."

> The notion of a free play of the mind upon all subjects being a
> pleasure in itself, being an object of desire, being an essential
> provider of elements without which a nation's spirit, whatever
> compensations it may have for them, must, in the long run, die
> of inanition, hardly enters into an Englishman's thoughts. It is
> noticeable that the word *curiosity*, which in other languages is
> used in a good sense, to mean, as a high and fine quality of
> man's nature, just this disinterested love of a free play of the
> mind on all subjects, for its own sake,—it is noticeable, I say,
> that this word has in our language no sense of the kind, no
> sense but a rather bad and disparaging one.[1]

The movement of Arnold's thought itself suggests what might
be "bad and disparaging" about curiosity. It is as if, waxing
eloquent about "free play," "pleasure," and particularly the
idea of the mind as its own "object of desire," Arnold is
momentarily (as he earlier says of Burke in a similar expression of rhetorical exuberance) "irresistibly carried . . . to the
opposite side of the question," thereby so forgetting the
"function" of criticism that he must recall himself to the matter
at hand: "It is noticeable . . . it is noticeable, I say." As Arnold

---

1. A. Dwight Culler, ed., *The Poetry and Criticism of Matthew Arnold* (Bos-
ton: Riverside, 1961), p. 245. Subsequent references are included in the text.

continues, curiosity—interest for its own sake—becomes "disinterestedness," and, by employing this more coldly complex term, criticism can abandon its ties with the practical and, paradoxically, get down to business. "Its business is, as I have said, simply to know the best that is known and thought in the world. . . . Its business is to do this with inflexible honesty . . . its business is to do no more" (246).

"He is neither comic nor tragic," writes Cesare Pavese of Balzac; "he is curious. He enters an entanglement of things, with the air of one who scents and promises a mystery. . . . Observe how he approaches his new characters: he scrutinizes them like rarities, defines, sculpts, and annotates them." "The fictional object does not appear alone," notes Pierre Macherey; "it is entangled, inscribed in the text which uses it, a token for something else, to herald its next impulse, constantly extending it into something else."[2] As a mode curiosity subordinates content to form; what is discovered matters less than the act of discovery, the constant extension from one thing to the next. And it is neither comic nor tragic because its primary interest lies in its own processes rather than in any particular object or situation. Like sentimentality and melodrama, curiosity entails, in Peter Brooks's words, "an excess of feeling in respect to situation," an exaggeration "more and more in and of consciousness itself."[3]

The *Oxford English Dictionary* also describes curiosity as excess. Curiosity is "undue niceness or fastidiousness"; "unduly minute or subtle treatment"; "the disposition to inquire too minutely into anything; undue or inquisitive desire to know or learn." It is self-reflexive—a curiosity's main characteristic is its curiosity—and nosy: "the habit of inquisitiveness as to trifles, and especially as to the private affairs of one's neighbors." These definitions suggest that our interest in others may be simply an overflow or displacement of our interest in

2. Pierre Macherey, *A Theory of Literary Production* (London: Routledge and Kegan Paul, 1978), p. 57.

3. Peter Brooks, *The Melodramatic Imagination* (New Haven: Yale University Press, 1976), pp. 177–78.

ourselves, and, further, that "looking into other people's affairs and overlooking our own," as the *OED* puts it, we register not only interest, but also the nature of the details we prefer to keep from the curious eyes of others. The object of curiosity serves as a kind of projective surface, telling us more about the curious agent than it does about itself. It is with this in mind that I turn to the discussion of a novel that comes to us surrounded by what is in effect the autobiography of its narrator, yet which purports, in its opening pages, to turn its attention entirely to the affairs of others.

Critics have often found *The Old Curiosity Shop* resonant with greater energy than its plot or characters manage to absorb. Criticism of the novel often remains bound, therefore, by the biographical circumstances of its creation.[4] The reasons for this are perhaps obvious. The Dickensian configuration of old man and young girl appears here in perhaps its purest form, and Dickens himself unabashedly alluded to what the story was "about": "Dear Mary died today, when I think of this sad story" (Forster, I:187). Without necessarily involving the explicit terms of Dickens's attachment to Mary Hogarth, critics remain concerned with the eroticization of Nell, the imagery and significance surrounding her death, and, in general, the balance between the figures of Nell and Quilp—a pairing that frequently depends upon a notion of the darker or demonic side of the author himself. Such readings place Dickens on the Quilpian side of the equation, associating him with the devouring energy that pursues Nell and finally drives her, sadistically, to death. Without completely abandoning the bio-

---

4. See, for example, Gabriel Pearson, "*The Old Curiosity Shop*," in John Gross and Gabriel Pearson, eds., *Dickens and the Twentieth Century* (Toronto: University of Toronto Press, 1962): "The reason why Nell offends more notoriously than Oliver is that so much significance is being read into her, and all so unsupported by anything she does or suffers. Ultimately, like Oliver, she remains a blank. . . . But, unlike Oliver, a great deal is being claimed for her, by lyrical commentary, by other characters, and by a structure that treats her death as a climax" (79). For reviews of *Old Curiosity Shop* criticism, see George Ford, *Dickens and His Readers* (Princeton: Princeton University Press, 1955), pp. 59–71; and Loralee MacPike, "The Old Cupiosity Shape," *Dickens Studies Newsletter* 12 (1981): 33–38 and 70–76.

graphical but rather changing the manner of its use, I would like to suggest another as yet unconsidered context for the novel, one which places it within the ongoing critical discussion of the Dickensian narrator's relation to, and position within, his narration.

Dickens is generally, and accurately, described as insistently present in his works. The energy and enthusiasm he invested in his public readings attest to his desire to confront an audience in person. Perhaps the most widely accepted account of his narratorial presence, Robert Garis's *Dickens Theatre*, ascribes such activity, as well as the flamboyant, performative quality of Dickens's language, to pure egotism. Dickens calls attention away from his characters and toward his own language, argues Garis, not only refusing, but unable, to grant his characters a separate, "inner" life. Other, less morally charged accounts describe the narrator's position in terms of increasing or decreasing involvement. J. Hillis Miller traces the narrator's movement from an inward, isolated position to an outward, social stance, while Taylor Stoehr suggests that the narrator becomes present in his work through a metonymic identification with his subject. But, as we have seen, Dickens's novels display a continual tension between inward and outward, impersonal and personal, present and absent stances. Dickens's insistent narratorial presence, especially his assertions of omniscient knowledge and mobility, conflict with the invisibility omniscience requires.[5]

Identification itself is a complicated and multifarious thing. While "part" of Dickens surely inhabits the demonic Quilp, another part of him flees in the form of Nell. Idealization involves both distance and involvement, presence and absence; the fantasized image of a loved one involves self-projection. (Thus David Copperfield's supposedly mature love for Agnes strongly involves an image of his best, what he

---

5. See Garis, *The Dickens Theatre*; J. Hillis Miller, *Charles Dickens: The World of His Novels* (Cambridge: Harvard University Press, 1957); Stoehr, *Dickens: The Dreamer's Stance*; Garrett, *The Victorian Multiplot Novel*; and Maxwell, "Dickens's Omniscience."

calls his most "earnest," self: "I only knew that I was fervently in earnest, when I felt the rest and peace of having Agnes near me.") Pursuer and pursued are interdependent, and *The Old Curiosity Shop* is about this interdependence and inseparability. In both its story and its narrative structurre, the novel bears the traces of the narrator's desire to free himself from what he is inextricably bound up with: to get out from inside. Beginning as a first-person narrative but quickly shifting to third-person omniscience, replacing autobiographical narration with curiosity about others, it invites us to explore the genesis and problematics of Dickensian omniscience. In particular, it allows us to examine the way in which omniscient narration, like curiosity, represents a displacement rather than a disappearance—the hiding, but not the removal, of the self.

At the end of *The Old Curiosity Shop*'s third chapter, the personified narrator (the dwarflike Humphrey of *Master Humphrey's Clock*, the serial out of which the novel grew) takes leave of his readers in order to let the novel's main characters "speak and act for themselves" (72). One hears nothing more of such a narrator until the novel's end when, in the continuation of the *Clock*, Humphrey announces that he has in fact been present all along in the person of the mysterious "single gentleman" who pursues Nell throughout the latter half of the book. Though editors tend to discount this "confession," as Humphrey calls it, it suggests what I want to claim for the book as a whole: that the status of the narrator—whether he is "in" or "out"—is not fully settled by his departure. The abandonment of personified in favor of omniscient narration suggests the need to gain the kind of distance, for the purposes of narration, that a character in the text can never attain. Omniscience, with its implications of superior knowledge and freedom, presumably signifies the narrator's achieved distance from the novel's characters, the ability to move invisibly among and outside them. Yet, in this novel, omniscience is a presence that neither readers nor characters are allowed to forget, and curiosity, I will argue, has a particular significance as Dickens's name for the narrator's relation to his characters: not the unproblematic achievement of distance and detachment, but rather a blurring of the boundaries that define and separate narrator and narration, subject and object.

In both *Master Humphrey's Clock* and *The Old Curiosity Shop*, the story of the narrator competes with, and threatens to displace, the stories he tells. Dickens intended the *Clock* only as a "machinery" or frame that would give continuity to a series of short pieces. Humphrey and his friends, meeting regularly to read their compositions to one another, were to serve as models for the reader rather than as "active agents in the stories they are supposed to relate."[6] (Imagining them "in their old chamber of meeting, eager listeners to all he had to tell, the Author hoped—as authors will—to succeed in awakening some of his own interest in the bosoms of his readers" [Preface, 339].) Yet the storytellers themselves embody stories, or "personal histories," as Dickens calls them, which need to be "wound up" before any other story can be told, and throughout the serial, the frame and its contents exist in a precarious balance, the personal histories of the storytellers often taking up as much room as, and appearing even more intriguing to their creator than, the tales to which they are ostensibly subordinated. Through oblique references to what he cannot or will not explain, Dickens piques the reader's curiosity about these partially given lives: "The reader must not expect to know where I live," begins Humphrey (*MHC*, 5). Even more oddly, after a tale has been read anonymously, its author reveals himself, "confessing" that the narrative actually describes some portion of his own experience, just as Humphrey confesses to a role in the *Curiosity Shop*. The third-person narrative is thus acknowledgedly, though secretly, autobiographical; the story of the other is in fact the story of the self.

6. Preface to the first volume of *Master Humphrey's Clock*, in *Edwin Drood* and *Master Humphrey's Clock*, vol. 33 of *The Works of Charles Dickens*, National Edition (London: Chapman and Hall, 1908), p. 338. All subsequent quotations from the preface are drawn from this edition and will be identified in the text by the word "preface" immediately preceding a page number. References to the text of *Master Humphrey's Clock* are to the Oxford edition (see Note on Editions) and are identified in the text by the abbreviation *MHC*.

What does this combination of story and "personal history" mean? What is the difference between telling one's story openly, in the first person, and telling it in the third person, followed by a "confession"? As he returns his own narrative to the clock case, Humphrey suggests a possible answer.

> I replaced in the clock case the record of so many trials,—sorrowfully, it is true, but with a softened sorrow that was almost pleasure; and felt that in living through the past again, and communicating to others the lesson it had helped to teach me, I had been a happier man. (*MHC*, 106)

"I can look back on my part in it," he claims, "with a calm, half-smiling pity for myself *as for some other man*" (*MHC*, 105, emphasis mine). Telling his story as if it belongs to another is, for Humphrey, a way of distancing painful feeling, of disowning a part of his experience so that he can, as narrator, indulge in that "softened sorrow that was almost pleasure." But the "as" peculiarly refuses either to merge or to separate the narrating from the participating self. It suggests the narrator's desire to disown his personal history, yet at the same time to remain its central actor.

The very existence of such narratorial figures as Boz and Humphrey bespeaks a desire to tell the narrator's story as well as that of what he observes. As the *Curiosity Shop* began to develop alongside *Master Humphrey's Clock*, Dickens briefly attempted to make room for both, writing Forster: "What do you think of the following double title for the beginning of that little tale? 'Personal Adventures of Master Humphrey: The Old Curiosity Shop'" (Forster, I:178). And, when the "little tale" started to crowd out its frame, he expressed his disappointment, letting readers know what they were missing.

> When the story was finished, that it might be freed from the incumbrances of associations and interruptions with which it had no kind of concern, I caused the few sheets of Master Humphrey's Clock, which had been printed in connection with it, to be cancelled. . . . Though I now affect to make the confession philosophically, as referring to a bye-gone emotion, I am conscious that my pen winces a little even as I write these words. But it was done, and wisely done, and Master Hum-

phrey's Clock, as originally constructed, became one of the lost
books of the earth—which, we all know, are far more precious
than any that can be read for love or money.
(Preface to the 1848 edition of
The Old Curiosity Shop)

In its movement from "bye-gone emotion" to "philosophical
confession," related to what sounds like a cutting away of part
of the self, this passage contains, in miniature, the substance
of my argument about *The Old Curiosity Shop*. The self is pain-
fully excised to produce a more "philosophical" narration:
someone else's story. But this excision merely gives rise to a
series of further displacements in which the story of the self is
told, over and over, as another's. And this series of displacements accounts for the novel's narrative structure, and for the
phenomenon of the narrator motivated solely by curiosity.

The desire to experience and discuss painful emotion
"philosophically," and even with pleasure, reappears in descriptions of Dickens's measured response to Mary Hogarth's
death. Steven Marcus writes: "After the first shock of Mary
Hogarth's death had worn off, Dickens wrote her mother that
he intended never to behave as if her memory were to be
avoided; he would never shrink from speaking of her; he was
determined to 'take a melancholy pleasure in recalling the
times when we were all so happy.'" He made that remembering into what Marcus calls a "ritual," dreaming of Mary every
night for the nine months following her death with "a kind of
quiet happiness, which became so pleasant to me that I never
lay down at night without a hope of the vision coming back in
one shape or other."[7] As "ritual," this obsessive recalling resembles Humphey's habitual curiosity, which has him indulg-
ing nightly and with apparent enjoyment in melancholy reflections, as well as his circle of companions in the *Clock*,
whose stories, regularly recounted, console them for the disappointments of actual life. The determined or deliberate calling up of emotion here involves a practice or rehearsal of

---

7. Steven Marcus, *Dickens: From Pickwick to Dombey* (London: Chatto and
Windus, 1965), p. 160. Subsequent references are included in the text.

feeling, as if to indulge and control it at the same time, and to demonstrate to oneself that it is controlled.[8] More important, this kind of rehearsal attempts to come to terms with the object of concern by substituting obsessive form ("ritual") for obsessive content, "philosophical confession" or narration for strong emotion. The narrator or dreamer, making the dream come and go as he pleases, imagines that he has gained control over his obsessive object and freed himself from the pain connected with it, but the very repetitiveness of his activity attests to his inability to do so. Instead, he has taken as his object the image of his own desire—a frozen, unattainable object—which he pursues relentlessly and, as with any self-projection, hopelessly. And throughout *The Old Curiosity Shop*, curiosity—while apparently directed toward others—is in fact self-projective, self-perpetuating, and potentially endless. Referring to an external object, it nonetheless proceeds with self-generated, directionless energy, just as, repeatedly declaring its pursuit of Nell, the narrative of *The Old Curiosity Shop* seems wandering, aimless, and potentially unending.[9]

What, then, am I claiming about the relationship between biography and fictional representation? Not that there is no actual event—such as Mary Hogarth's death—behind *The Old Curiosity Shop*, but that we can understand that event as a kind of vessel or clock-case out of which narratives are drawn, providing an opportunity for fictional displacement rather than standing as the essence or source of any particular story.

The first few chapters of the novel struggle, and fail, to maintain a balance between the narrator and his ostensible object; Humphrey then "disappears," and the *Curiosity Shop* alone becomes our concern. Yet the distance the narrator hopes to gain by choosing omniscient over personified narration is repeatedly undermined by the narrative's persistent

8. Richard O. Allen sees this process as characteristic of sentimentality: "If You Have Tears: Sentimentalism as Soft Romanticism," *Genre* 8 (1975): 119–45.

9. For discussions of the relationship between self-projection and the desire that generates narrative, see René Girard, *Deceit, Desire, and the Novel* (Baltimore: Johns Hopkins University Press, 1965); and Angela S. Moger, "That Obscure Object of Narrative," *Yale French Studies* 63 (1982): 139–48.

focus on an analogous movement within the novel: figures who strive for, but cannot attain, positions outside scenes in which they are involved. *The Old Curiosity Shop* repeatedly focuses on observational activity, shifting from an unframed, central action to an observer on the periphery of that action. The best example is the dilemma presented by Humphrey himself, who, after alluding to his deformity and habit of walking at night, attempts to take his place as an observer of others, with the idea that he must not, much as he would like to, tell his own story. Yet he cannot so easily abandon his participatory role; his departure becomes a competition of curiosities between himself and Nell. Having made her the object of his curiosity, that is, he nevertheless begins, and with increasing anxiety, to notice her noticing of him. "I observed that every now and then she stole a curious look at my face as if to make sure that I was not deceiving her . . ."; "my curiosity and interest were at least equal to the child's . . ."; "her quick eye seemed to read my thoughts . . ." (45). The same thing occurs when Humphrey meets Nell's grandfather, and then Quilp: each character he observes manifests—according to Humphrey—a significant degree of interest in him. This reciprocal curiosity reflects the awkwardness of Humphrey's narratorial position, but it also defines his departure as a retreat from the curiosity of others, as if the narrator cannot be present in the text without threatening to displace its proper object. Like the novel's recurrent notice of spying, it suggests the observer's desire to be the focus of curiosity, the possibility that his excessive interest in others represents the displacement of an interest he desires for himself.

Humphrey's encounter with Nell is only the first in a series of instances in which a curious observer finds himself becoming an object of curiosity—in which the narrative suddenly points toward a figure who, often unbeknownst to readers and other characters, has been lingering at its edges. Soon after Humphrey's departure, for example, as Nell encourages her grandfather to leave town with her, we learn that "these were not words for other ears, nor was it a scene for other eyes. And yet other ears and eyes were there and greedily taking in all that passed, and moreover they were the ears and eyes of no less a person than Mr. Daniel Quilp" (124). Quilp has planted himself inside the shop, of which he is soon to take complete possession, displacing its original owners. This narrative shift from the inner scene to its periphery disrupts the reader's unmediated involvement, effectively displacing him or her by framing the inner scene, making it the object of another character's attention. At the same time Quilp becomes both subject and object of the reader's gaze; seeing what he sees, we suddenly see him as well. And that movement repeats itself almost immediately: "Daniel Quilp," we are told, "neither entered nor left the old man's house, unobserved" (129); Kit now watches from the corner. Humphrey's departure therefore plays out only the initial version of a tension between subject and object that continues to inform much of the narrative, calling the stability of each term into question and keeping the reader always slightly off balance. For as it sets each scene within a larger scene, or series of scenes, the novel underscores the limitations of any representable point of view. Trapped within this infinite regress, no character can achieve an authoritative perspective. And the concern with limitation extends, by means of its very insistence, to the narrator himself; the spy who uncovers another's spying implicitly acknowledges his own vulnerability. An omniscience that makes itself felt is thus on the defensive, protesting its outside stance because it is caught inside.

Within such a framework, there can be no successful overview. Instead, the narrative mimes Nell's journey. Taking note of what immediately surrounds the travelers, it can posit only vagueness ahead and increasing vagueness behind.

> At length these streets, becoming more straggling yet, dwindled and dwindled away, until there were only small garden patches bordering the road. . . . To these succeeded pert cottages. . . . Then came the public house, freshly painted . . . then fields . . . then came a turnpike; then fields again . . . then a hill; and on top of that the traveller might stop, and— looking back at old Saint Paul's looming through the smoke, its cross peeping above the cloud . . . casting his eyes upon the

> Babel out of which it grew until he traced it down to the
> furthest outposts of the invading army of bricks and mortar
> whose station lay for the present nearly at his feet—might feel
> at last that he was clear of London. (173)

As the two leave London, the city is something "a traveller
might see," a blurred "Babel" recognizable chiefly by its sign:
the top of Saint Paul's. From within the novel it is almost
impossible to see more than what immediately surrounds one.
Hence narratorial surrogates like Quilp must keep popping up
directly alongside their intended victims.

The difficulty of separating subject from object appears not
only in the novel's narrative structure, but also in the meaning
of curiosity itself, which throughout the novel displaces observed with observer. The habitual nature of Humphrey's
night-walking reveals a great deal, notably that curiosity—an
ostensibly spontaneous, unpredictable response—takes place
regularly, at the observer's instigation. Its self-generated, habitual quality becomes clearly evident as Humphrey wonders
about Nell's grandfather's nighttime activities:

> What could have taken him from home by night, and every
> night! I called up all the strange tales I had ever heard of dark
> and secret deeds committed in great towns and escaping detec-
> tion. (55)

Humphrey's curiosity has an obsessive quality about it:

> [A]ll that night . . . the same thoughts recurred and the same
> images retained possession of my brain. (56)

But independence from the object of curiosity means eternal
failure to capture it. Curiosity turns in on itself, its object—
Nell or her grandfather—merely the catalyst for a fantasy
which ultimately cannot distinguish between projection and
external reality. It makes sense, then, that the narrative itself
fails to distinguish self from other, that it confuses Humphrey's habitual speculations with what might be the representations of others' thoughts.

> Think of a sick man . . . listening to the footsteps, and in
> the midst of pain and weariness obliged, despite himself (as

though it were a task he must perform) to detect the child's step from the man's. . . . [T]hink of the hum and noise being always present to his senses, and of the stream of life that will not stop, pouring on, on, on, through all his restless dreams. (43)[10]

[M]any stop on fine evenings looking listlessly down upon the water with some vague idea that by-and-by it runs between green banks which grow wider and wider until at last it joins the broad vast sea—where some halt to rest from heavy loads and think as they look over the parapet that to smoke and lounge away one's life, and lie sleeping in the sun . . . must be happiness unalloyed—and where some, of a very different class, pause with heavier loads than they, remembering to have heard or read in some old time that drowning was not a hard death, but of all means of suicide the easiest and best. (43–44)

Critics typically attribute the thoughts of these restless and depressed passersby to Humphrey, but the narrative deliberately invites the possibility that they belong to others. Curiosity remains unable to separate subject from object, and that failure underlies the movement of this narrative. The mystery, Humphrey asserts, "only became the more impenetrable, in proportion as I sought to solve it" (55). "Every effort I made to penetrate it," insists the single gentleman, "has only served to render it darker and more obscure" (367).[11] The narrative's economy depends upon the unattainability of its object, which moves ahead in equal measure with the desire for it. The mind thus produces fantasy rather than seeking an end to it, as one of Dickens's manuscript emendations reveals. Originally, when Humphrey queries Nell as to what she has been doing wandering the streets at night, she replies, "Selling diamonds." In the revision, her answer reads, "That, I must not tell"—announcing the existence of a secret and the need for further questions (682, note 3).

What does it mean, in this context, for a narrator to detach

10. The need to "detect the child's step from the man's" is significant. In *Master Humphrey's Clock*, Humphrey speaks of wandering about his house and hearing in his own footsteps "the light step of some lovely girl" (5).

11. The novel's sexual undertones have received much attention. See, for example, Meredith Skura, *The Literary Uses of the Psychoanalytic Process* (New Haven: Yale University Press, 1981), pp. 113–24 and 190–99.

himself from his tale—to get outside it? *Master Humphrey's Clock* suggests an answer in what apppears to be an originary scene for *The Old Curiosity Shop*, one which reverses the novel's initiating image of Nell in the shop surrounded by curiosities. Humphrey recounts his discovery of his deformity in this scene, which has him—the ugly dwarf—surrounded by "angels."

> A little knot of playmates—they must have been beautiful, for I see them now—were clustered around my mother's knee in eager admiration of some picture representing a group of infant angels, which she held in her hand. . . . I have some dim thought it was my birthday. . . . There were many lovely angels in this picture, and I remember the fancy coming upon me to point out which of them represented each child there, and that when I had gone through my companions, I stopped and hesitated, wondering which was most like me. I remember the children looking at each other, and my turning red and hot, and their crowding around to kiss me, saying they loved me all the same; and then, when the old sorrow came into my dear mother's mild and tender look, the truth broke upon me for the first time, and I knew, while watching my awkward and ungainly sports, how keenly she had felt for her poor crippled boy. (*MHC*, 8)

Buried within this passage are two sorrows: the death of Humphrey's mother and that of his earliest image of himself. Yet he introduces the passage as another "philosophical confession," a recollection of happy moments with his mother, who died when he was young. "I smile sorrowfully to think," he writes, "that the time has been when the confession would have given me pain" (*MHC*, 7). Lacan's account of early childhood development describes the child's inability to differentiate his own image from his mother's, as well as the simultaneity of self-recognition and self-alienation in the mirror stage.[12] Here, self-recognition entails self-displacement, as

---

12. See "The Mirror Stage" and "Aggressivity in Psychoanalysis," both in *Ecrits*, as well as Anika Lemaire's *Jacques Lacan* (London: Routledge and Kegan Paul, 1977), ch. 7. "In the other, in the mirror image, in his mother, the child sees nothing but a fellow with whom he merges, with whom he identifies" (Lemaire, p. 78). "It is in this erotic relation [between the ego and its two

Humphrey's ambiguous sentence structure implies: "*I* knew, while watching [my sports] . . . how keenly *she* had felt. . . ." Suddenly seeing himself as if from the outside—already a displacement—the child just as suddenly disowns his painful feeling, becoming the story's invisible narrator rather than its shamed object, as the passage focuses exclusively on his mother's expression. And, as he continues his narrative, Humphrey distances himself even further from his own image: "I used frequently to dream of it afterwards," he writes, "and now my heart aches for that child *as if I had never been he,* when I think how often he awoke from some fairy change to his own form, and sobbed himself to sleep again" (*MHC,* 9, my emphasis).[13] Each awakening involves both a death and a birth, the death of "that child" and the birth of the detached narrator—a detachment which, one might say, reflects the child's initial lack of reflection: his inability to find a self-representation in his mother's book.

The structure and resolution of this passage—its movement from pride in being the center of attention ("I have some dim thought it was my birthday") to sudden shame and displacement of feeling—recall a passage in Dickens's "Autobiographical Fragment." When Warren's Blacking moves into larger quarters, Dickens and his fellow workers find themselves tying pots of Bootblack near a window, in public view. "Bob Fagin and I had attained to great dexterity in tying up the pots," Dickens writes.

> I forget how many we could do, in five minutes. We worked, for the light's sake, near the second window as you come from Bedford street; and we were so brisk at it, that the people used

---

objects], in which the human individual fixes upon himself an image that alienates him from himself . . ." (Lacan, p. 19).

13. In "Relationships of Person in the Verb" and "Subjectivity in Language" (both in *Problems of General Linguistics*), Benveniste discusses the use of the third person to express detachment and non-being: "the third person is not a 'person'; it is really the verbal form whose function it is to express the *'non-person'* " (198). For Benveniste, self-consciousness exists only in relation to an "other," and the subjective self comes into being only through alienation: "Consciousness of self is only possible if it is experienced by contrast" (224).

to stop and look in. Sometimes there would be quite a little crowd there. I saw my father coming in at the door one day when we were very busy, and I wondered how he could bear it.

(Forster, I:48)

Again, pride—a desire to be looked at—becomes shame, anxiety about being looked at. The moment of discovery is a moment of refusal, of experience transformed into what Dickens so often calls "personal history." In the first passage, the "red and hot" child becomes the cool observer of his mother's "old sorrow." Here, he "wonders" why his father doesn't feel the shame that, the "Fragment" fully attests, actually belongs to the son. As in *The Old Curiosity Shop*, the narrator turns against others the gaze that had been focused on him, displacing or even excising its accompanying feeling. The subject of the text is no longer the object of gazes.[14]

These moments demonstrate the production and characteristic form of the Dickens narrator, moving between omniscience and character, existing shadowlike within his text. So, at various points in *Master Humphrey's Clock*, Humphrey imagines his death as a transition beyond the bounds of self and speaks of "hovering, the ghost of his former self, about the places and people that warmed his heart of old." Death means not absence, but attendant presence: "If my spirit should ever glide back to this chamber when my body is mingled with the dust, it will but follow the course it took in *the old man*'s lifetime, and add but one more change to the subjects of his contemplation" (*MHC*, 33, emphasis mine). This "contemplation" has consequences, moreover, for his onetime associates. Humphrey's will enjoins that his companions preserve his apartments, belongings, and portrait as they were during his lifetime, and, further, that they make him a frequent subject of conversation, never speaking of him "with an air of gloom or restraint, but frankly, as one whom we still loved and hoped to meet again" (*MHC*, 117). Though a number of characters in *The Old Curiosity Shop* exercise control over others through

14. See the discussion of this scene by Robert Newsom in "The Hero's Shame," *Dickens Studies Annual* 11 (1983): 12–14.

absence—one need only think of the compelling power of Nell's image, or the schoolmaster's obsession with his dead student—Humphrey's fantasy of invisible presence most disturbingly resembles Quilp's means of keeping his wife, mother-in-law, and in fact almost every character in the novel perpetually on guard simply by posing the threat of his presence. When, after he has been absent for several days, his family and cohorts imagine him drowned, Quilp returns in the midst of a conversation about himself, delighting in "the prospect of playing the spy under such delicious circumstances, and of disappointing them all by walking in alive" (457). From that point on, he determines fully to inhabit the role he has only hinted at until then, keeping his wife and mother-in-law in "a constant state of agitation and suspense" by keeping them unadvised of his whereabouts: "I'll be a spy upon you, and come and go like a mole or a weazel" (464).

Humphrey's interest in Nell, we have seen, is ambivalent from the start. His concern for her is an afterthought to his excitement about her as "riddle," an excitement oddly unaligned with sympathy. As Nell chats with him, Humphrey "revolved in my mind a hundred different explanations of the riddle and rejected them every one. I really felt ashamed to take advantage of the ingenuousness or grateful feeling of the child for the purpose of gratifying my curiosity" (46). He even attributes to her a desire to deceive him, which he then counters by deceiving her, leading her in a circuitous route she will not recognize. But while Humphrey's narrative role requires an awkward invasion of privacy (he must return to the shop, gain entrance for no particular reason, and, once inside, sit passively by recording what takes place), omniscient narration can infiltrate the text without acknowledgment, since it is ostensibly a neutral, invisible activity—the novelist's business. As if to offset this neutrality, however, an image of evil omniscience appears. Humphrey's ambivalent curiosity and correspondingly awkward visitations to the shop are replaced by Quilp's deliberate, aggressive spying: he steals into it, unobserved, to overhear Nell's conversation. Narratorial intrusiveness is objectified, domesticated, absorbed into the necessities of plot; omniscient narration detaches itself from, and vilifies, a curiosity it no longer calls its own. Quilp embodies the sinister potential of a curiosity that only lingers at the edges of Humphrey's speculations.

Nell is "constantly haunted by a vision of his ugly face and stunted figure" (288), and other characters experience similar "hauntings." During his illness, Dick Swiveller "senses some fearful obstacle to be surmounted . . . recognizable for the same phantom in every shape it took" (579). Kit, in prison, dreams

> always of being at liberty, and roving about, now with one person and now with another; but ever with a vague dread of being recalled to prison; not that prison, but one which was itself a dim idea, not of a place, but of a care and sorrow; of something oppressive and always present, and yet impossible to define. (557)

The phantom that is always present but impossible to define; that resembles a prison but is not a place; that keeps characters semiconscious of the need to find someplace secure and hidden and at the same time aware of the impossibility of doing so: this sounds like omniscient observation provided characters could be aware of it.

Quilp is finally displaced, as other observers have been. The novel defeats him, replacing one observer with another: the Marchioness, spying on him and the Brasses, discovers their plot against Kit. His death, which Dickens represents as a failure of vision, resembles as well a failure of omniscient powers. After Sally warns him that the game is up, Quilp sees the dense mist as a welcome cover: "a good night for travelling anonymously" (617). But the capacity for anonymous travel that has served him in the past hinders him now, for the mist hides him from his potential rescuers. "[T]hey were all but looking on while he drowned . . . they were close at hand, but could not make an effort to save him. . . . he himself had shut and barred them out" (620).

The focus of almost every character's observation and interest is, of course, Nell. Nell seems "to exist in a kind of alle-

gory" (56), throughout the novel frequently signifying something other than herself. From the book's opening moments,
when Humphrey questions her in the street, her significance
lies in where she will lead, and her own journey is structured
in relation to what lies "beyond." Each place in which she and
her grandfather stop is on the way to some vague elsewhere:
"Places lie beyond these," she says characteristically, urging
him ahead. As Humphrey's initial, dreamlike fantasy about
her suggests, Nell is a product of curiosity, inseparable from
the idea of pursuit or of desire for her. "It would be a curious
speculation," Humphrey muses, "to imagine her in her future
life, holding her solitary way among a crowd of wild grotesque
companions. . . . [I]t would be curious to find—" (56).

Thus while the novel is committed to Nell's inviolability
and purity, it is also continually involved in the attempt to
uncover her, to violate her privacy. And while such language
suggests that the novel is grounded in a desire for sexual
violation, even that idea involves the paradox that the novel
be dedicated to uncovering what it also wants to preserve. In
fact, the novel finally protects Nell by keeping whatever she is
separate from what others perceive her to be. Generations of
critics have agreed that Nell represents essential values of
youth, goodness, and truth, but they have not remarked that
she also provides a vehicle for the fantasies of each character
who desires or is curious about her. Her grandfather, for
example, uses her to justify his gambling. Even though he
seems to believe that he will eventually make her rich, his
obsession obviously does not depend upon her presence. The
idea of his miserliness emerges from Quilp's misinterpretation
of Nell's secret, which Fred Trent seizes upon, making Dick
Swiveller part of his scheme to gain the old man's wealth
through marriage to Nell. For Dick, Nell is really only part of
Fred's plan, and incidentally a means of inspiring jealousy in
the recalcitrant Sophy Wackles. The single gentleman sees in
her a way of reclaiming the woman he loved two generations
past but gave up to his brother, and for him her sameness does
not signify purity or goodness, but simply reflects that past.
She is "the same sweet girl [one traces] through a line of

portraits, never growing old or changing . . . the same in helplessness, in age, in form, in feature" (637). For the school-master, she embodies the dead little scholar, "as if my love for him who died, had been transferred to you who stood beside his bed" (435). For Mrs. Jarley, she constitutes the waxworks' main "attraction," while for Codlin and Short, she again repre-sents wealth, namely, the possibility of a reward for her return to wherever she came from. Even for Kit, Nell embodies a fantasy of perfect service and devotion, connected with an image of his best self. Nell is to be always "just as she used to be," and Kit "always . . . what I should like to seem to her if I was still her servant" (632). Nell and her grandfather are cre-ated anew by each character that observes them, precisely because they appear to have no content or direction them-selves. Both as a couple and against the landscape, they pre-sent an odd juxtaposition, a cognitive gap, which requires explanation and generates fantasy. As Humphrey suggests early in the novel, the contrast between Nell and her sur-roundings serves as a "visible aid" to "reflection" (56).

The idea that interest, and narrative, arise around places of secrecy or absence has corollaries throughout the novel and in *Master Humphrey's Clock*. The notion of being an invisible cen-ter of interest, as I suggested earlier, forms an essential part of Humphrey's fantasy about himself.

> When I first came to live here, which was many years ago, the neighbours were curious to know who I was, and whence I came, and why I lived so much alone. As time went on, and they still remained unsatisfied on these points, I became the center of a popular ferment, extending for half a mile round, and in one direction for a full mile. Various rumours were circulated to my prejudice. I was a spy, an infidel, a conjurer, a kidnapper of children, a refugee, a priest, a monster. . . . I was the object of suspicion and distrust—ay, of downright hatred too. (*MHC*, 6)

Interest in Nell takes a similarly geographical form. In the novel's final chapters, when she settles down under the bach-elor's care, she becomes an object of curiosity for the entire village: "humble folks for seven miles around . . . had an interest in Nell" (509). Throughout the novel, places where Nell has stopped become the sites of stories. Thus the workman who shelters the pair in his factory attaches "fresh interest to the spot where his guests had slept, and read new histories in his furnace fire" (422). When the single gentleman seeks her at Mrs. Jarley's, his interest sparks rumors

> that the little girl who used to show the wax-work, was the child of great people who had been stolen from her parents in infancy, and had only just been traced. Opinion was divided whether she was the daughter of a prince, a duke, an earl, a viscount, or a baron. (446)

And, when the schoolmaster encounters her for the second time, it is as "story" that he thinks of her. "[T]he world is full of such heroism. Have I yet to learn that the hardest and best-born trials are those which are never chronicled in any earthly record, and are suffered every day! And I should be surprised to hear the story of this child!" (435). Nell herself is a fascinated reader of gravestones, and after her death the narrative focuses on spots where she has been, and on the place of her death, as generative of further narrative.

Within the novel, art is conceived of as valuable to the extent that it remains hidden. Codlin calculates how much he has lost by Nell's coming upon Punch in disrepair: "Would you care a ha'penny for the Lord Chancellor if you know'd him in private and without his wig?—certainly not" (183). And Mrs. Jarley, especially concerned about the secrecy of her art, moves Nell indoors lest she become "too cheap" when the child becomes the waxworks' chief attraction.

Nell's seven miles of interest scarcely begin to describe the imaginative reach of the novel itself, of course. As is well known, the question of Nell's fate generated enormous curiosity, both in England and in America.[15] The idea of Nell as a vehicle for fantasy thus has a place in the story of the novel's publication. As I mentioned earlier, the novel itself was created because an audience asked for it. Within the novel, art is

15. See Ford, *Dickens and His Readers*, ch. 4.

not only valuable because of its secrecy, but to some extent takes shape as the product of an audience's desire and curiosity. Various forms of popular art described are "convertible": "Have the acrostic," says Mr. Slum. "Five shillings. . . . Cheaper than any prose." "[T]he name at this moment is Warren, but the idea's a convertible one, and a positive inspiration for Jarley" (282). Even the waxworks themselves are convertible. When presenting her exhibit at young ladies' boarding schools "of a very superior description," Mrs. Jarley transforms "the face and costume of Mr. Grimaldi as clown to represent Mr. Lindley Murray as he appeared when engaged in the composition of his English Grammar," and turns "a murderess of great renown into Miss Hannah More."

> Mr. Pitt in a nightcap and bedgown, and without his boots, represented the poet Cowper with perfect exactness, and Mary Queen of Scots in a dark wig, white shirt-collar, and male attire, was such a complete image of Lord Byron that the young ladies quite screamed when they saw it. (288)

In short, these passages may be read as a cynical commentary on the necessity of suiting popular art to its audience. The material of personal history ("The name at this moment is Warren"), already part of an "acrostic," can—with slight alterations—be attached to any name. Objects of popular admiration can be shaped this way or that in order to preserve their popularity. The novel thus comments on, and reflects, the quality of being shaped in part by an audience's desire.

But if art is depicted as malleable, narrative—and specifically storytelling—also play a role in keeping memories alive and in laying them to rest. A number of Dickens's works warn of the dangers of forgetting. *The Haunted Man* suggests that one can be whole only by remembering the bad as well as the good; *Little Dorrit*'s motto, "Do Not Forget," asserts the tortuous necessity of bad memories, both as a means of punishing the evil doer and of bringing about reparation for his deeds. The end of *The Old Curiosity Shop*, however, is about the dangers of obsessive remembering. The narrative continues beyond Nell's death, circling around her image, in various attempts to come to terms with it. While Humphrey wants to survive in the minds of the living, for Nell's survivors such presence is a kind of nightmare, leading to obsessive repetition that only death can end. The single gentleman accordingly begins an endless retreading of the path taken by Nell and her grandfather. As long as Nell's image remains in the minds of those who knew her, the narrative can do nothing, it seems, but pursue it. Her grandfather returns repeatedly to the "places of last sorrow," finally dying on Nell's gravestone. The grave itself becomes a site for storytelling.

> The service done, the mourners stood apart, and the villagers closed round to look into the grave before the pavement-stone should be replaced. One called to mind how he had seen her sitting on that very spot, and how her book had fallen on her lap, and she was gazing with a pensive face upon the sky. Another told, how he had wondered much that one so delicate as she, should be so bold; how she had never feared to enter the church alone at night. . . . A whisper went about among the oldest there, that she had seen and talked with angels. (658)

When Nell arrives at the churchyard which is to be her final destination, her appointed task is to guide tours, as she did for Mrs. Jarley—to recite the "personal histories" of the dead as instructed by the character known only as the "bachelor." (Like the other unnamed bachelors in the book, he evokes the absent Humphrey, who has similarly renounced his own history for the histories of others.) The bachelor is the historian of the churchyard, the preserver and in fact creator of its biographies, for in this churchyard only certain kinds of stories are permitted. Here, as Nell's grandfather says, "there are no dreams" (504); it is "another world, where sin and sorrow never came; a tranquil place of rest, where nothing evil entered" (498). And to maintain it as such, the bachelor "would have had every stone and plate of brass, the monument only of deeds whose memory should survive" (497). He

> was not one of those rough spirits who would strip fair Truth of every little shadowy vestment in which time and teeming fancies loved to array her—and some of which became her pleasantly enough, serving, like the waters of her well, to add new

graces to the charms they half conceal and half suggest. . . . [H]e trod with a light step and bore with a light hand upon the dust of centuries, unwilling to demolish any of the airy shrines that had been raised above it, if one good feeling or affection of the human heart were hiding thereabouts. (496–97)

Indeed, the bachelor's storytelling principle resembles Humphrey's. "We are alchemists who would extract the essence of perpetual youth from dust and ashes, tempt coy Truth in many light and airy forms from the bottom of her well, and discover one crumb of comfort or one grain of good in the commonest and least regarded matter that passes through our crucible" (*MHC*, 11). Thus the bachelor amends the stories of those whose graves he tends, so that, for example, "in the case of an ancient coffin of rough stone, supposed for many generations to contain the bones of a certain baron, who [ravaged] with cut, and thrust, and plunder, in foreign lands . . . the bachelor stoutly maintained that the old tale was the true one; that the baron, repenting him of the evil, had done great charities and meekly given up the ghost" (497). The bachelor valorizes narrative that softens and idealizes its object, surrounding it with fictions, and truth lies in the ameliorated story rather than the germ of fact at its core. Dickens dedicated *The Old Curiosity Shop*, it is worth recalling, to the poet Samuel Rogers, with particular reference to his poem "The Pleasures of Memory." In more fundamental ways, as I suggested earlier, the novel undertakes to replace unhappy memories with pleasant ones. Yet the insistence on burial and repression in both the bachelor's and Humphrey's formulations makes that transformation a disturbing one, an evasion rather than a working through, replacing the novel's principle of contrast—its alternation of good and evil, turmoil and tranquility—with an ideal of narrative, and death, as endless happy stories.[16]

16. "Contrast" is a frequent topic in the criticism, one which Dickens himself invites: "Everything in our lives, whether of good or evil, affects us most by contrast" (493). For an example, see A. E. Dyson, "*The Old Curiosity Shop*: Innocence and the Grotesque," in A. E. Dyson, ed., *Dickens: Modern Judgements* (London: Macmillan, 1968): 59–81.

Philip Rogers has argued that the novel forces Nell to acknowledge the grim reality of death through the character of
the old sexton, who compels her to look down a dry well,
which he calls a grave.[17] But truth's well, as both Humphrey
and the bachelor describe it, is hardly so dark and forbidding,
and the sexton seems to limit his willingness to face "reality"
to the realities of others. "[H]ow strange," thinks Nell, "that
this old man, drawing from his pursuits . . . one stern moral,
never contemplated its application to himself" (493). Rogers
claims that the novel rejects the bachelor's approach, pointing
out that the bachelor turns out to be Mr. Garland's brother,
and that the Garlands' idyllic life represents another "fearful
evasion" of "the decaying world Nell faces" (143). But it was
Dickens's stated intention to "substitute a garland of fresh
flowers for the sculptured horrors that disgrace the tomb,"[18]
and though Rogers is certainly correct about the Garlands'
evasiveness, Dickens himself, in his desire to remember the
dead frequently and with pleasure, resembles Humphrey and
the Garlands more than he does the hypocritical sexton.

Only Kit, in the novel's last moments, suggests a way of
ending its preoccupation with Nell's image, of laying the past
to rest. Returning to the spot that generated the novel—the
site of the curiosity shop—he stages what can be read as a

---

17. Philip Rogers, "The Dynamics of Time in *The Old Curiosity Shop*,"
Nineteenth Century Fiction 28 (1973): 127–44.

18. The phrase comes from a speech given in Edinburgh (25 June 1841):

When I first conceived the idea of conducting that simple story to its
termination, I determined rigidly to adhere to it, and never to forsake
the end I had in view. Not untried in the school of affliction, in the
death of those we love, I thought what a good thing it would be if in my
little work of pleasant amusement I could substitute a garland of fresh
flowers for the sculptured horrors that disgrace the tomb. If I have put
into my book anything which can fill the young mind with better
thoughts of death, or soften the grief of older hearts; if I have written
one word which can afford pleasure or consolation to old or young in
time of trial, I shall consider it as something achieved—something
which I shall be glad to look back upon in after life.

Speeches of Charles Dickens, ed. K. J. Fielding (Oxford:
Clarendon Press, 1960), p. 10.

commentary on the process of the narrative itself. The shop is gone, and "at first he would draw with his stick a square upon the ground to show them where it used to stand. But he soon became uncertain of the spot, and could only say that it was thereabouts, and that these alterations were confusing. Such are the changes which a few years bring about, and so do things pass away, like a tale that is told!" (671–72). Curiosity again misses its mark; narrative, it seems, can only express desire, and then nostalgia, for its object. The "tale" does not pass away—we have it before us—but the image that gave rise to it can begin to dissolve, and be replaced, through storytelling. Employing Nell's image as a lesson for the future, rather than as an unattainable reality, Kit tells a tale that manages to subordinate the past to the present and to separate Nell's image from his own. He tells his children

> how she had gone to Heaven, as all good people did; and how, if they were good like her, they might hope to be there too one day. . . . Then he would relate to them how needy he used to be, and how she had taught him what he was otherwise too poor to learn, and how the old man had been used to say 'she always laughs at Kit;' at which they would brush away their tears, and laugh to themselves to think that she had done so, and be again quite merry. (671)

Kit's mode of storytelling might serve as a model for the reader, or for Dickens's own "working through." Treating Nell as his children must—as legend—he incorporates her story into and subordinates it to his own, so that their tears are replaced (rather than displaced) by laughter. Though narrative might be said always to involve self-displacement—the disappearance of the narrating self—this story tells significantly of Nell *and* Kit, no longer of the pursuit of a fantasy Nell. Only such a story, one might argue, can successfully end the novel. Perhaps most important, Kit's story conveys a sense that present and continuing life outweighs past sorrows. Rather than sustaining Nell's image, the children's tears seem to disperse it, and the narrative itself finally seems subordinate to the life that goes on around it, learns from it, and will continue beyond it.

❨ 3 ❩

Dombey and Son
The World Within and the World Without

For all his starched, impenetrable dignity and composure,
he wiped blinding tears from his eyes as he paced up and
down his room; and often said, with an emotion of which he
would not, for the world, have had a witness, "Poor little
fellow!"

Dombey and Son

In *Dombey and Son*, as in all omnisciently narrated novels,
readers often see what characters wish to keep secret. Apparently disregarding boundaries between public and private
spheres, omniscience creates its characteristic effects precisely
by establishing and then violating such boundaries. But while
this is always true of omniscience, *Dombey*'s narrator reminds
us of it more often than most. Through comments such as the
above, through extended scenes in which we observe Florence
or Dombey alone, readers are made aware that they observe
scenes in which characters would, but for narrator and readers, remain unobserved.

Exposing private matters to the public eye, Dombey's narrator might seem to resemble the instrusive public world that
haunts Dombey after the scandal of Edith's departure and the
bankruptcy of the firm.

The world. What the world thinks of him, how it looks at him,
what it sees in him, and what it says—this is the haunting
demon of his mind. It is everywhere where he is; and, worse
than that, it is everywhere where he is not. It comes out with
him among his servants, and yet he leaves it whispering behind; he sees it pointing after him in the street; it is waiting for

> him in his counting house; it leers over the shoulders of rich
> men among the merchants; it goes beckoning and babbling
> among the crowd; it always anticipates him, in every place; and
> is always busiest, he knows, when he has gone away. When he
> is shut up in his room at night, it is in his house, outside it,
> audible in footsteps on the pavement, visible in print upon the
> table, steaming to and fro on railroads and in ships; restless and
> busy everywhere, with nothing else but him. (809)

How, we might ask, does the novel's omniscience differ from
this? Or from the curious strangers who, also after Dombey's
ruin, participate in the dismantling of his house?

> There is not a secret place in the whole house. Fluffy and snuffy
> strangers stare into the kitchen range as curiously as into the
> attic clothes-press. Stout men with napless hats on, look out of
> the bedroom windows, and cut jokes with friends in the street.
> (928)

The demise of the firm of Dombey and Son is accompanied by
the end of Dombey's ability to sustain his powerful public
image—to hide, as the novel puts it, "the world within him
from the world without" (808). But the novel's omniscience
has already revealed "the world within." Gossip and rumor,
we might argue, only expose what *Dombey*'s readers have
already been shown; publicity only seeks the violent effacement of boundaries the omniscient narrator has already, more
quietly, effaced. *Dombey*'s narrator in fact makes a point of
taking characters behind locked doors and pursuing them
there: "[H]e went into his room, and locked the door, and sat
down in his chair, and cried for his lost boy" (329). "When the
door yielded, and he rushed in, what did he see there? No one
knew. But thrown down in a costly mass upon the ground,
was every ornament she had had, since she had been his wife"
(756).

Yet even as the novel charts the destruction of Dombey's
private and public worlds, it differentiates its methods from
those of the public world, describing the latter as rapacious,
greedy, and careless about knowledge. Where gossip, rumor,
and publicity can only speculate, deriving their energy from
their lack of knowledge, omniscience is certain: "But this is

sure: he does *not* think that he has lost her. He has no suspicion of the truth" (808). And because it is sure of what takes place behind closed doors—because it so absolutely violates privacy—the novel's omniscience paradoxically manages to align itself against the public world and with the private, even as it reveals private affairs to the public eye.

Confiding to each reader what, it claims, "no one knows," *Dombey*'s narration provokes a peculiar double consciousness: a sense of privacy in the midst of publicity. In order to value the private sphere as it does, the novel must expose it, making what occurs in private a kind of demonstration of privacy, putting privacy into circulation. Omniscience, with its emphasis on interiority, its interest in revealing what transpires when "no one" is present—its ability, precisely, to violate privacy—is paradoxically suited to disseminate the values of private life: to sustain a fiction of privacy.

As it publicizes the private, the novel opposes privacy to the public business world, a world represented as requiring the deformation or management of natural feeling—one where, as Mr. Carker the Manager puts it, "our interest and convenience commonly oblige many of us to make professions we cannot feel" (717). Writing on what she calls the "commercialization of human feeling," Arlie Russell Hochschild discusses the way in which emotions, when required for the performance of labor, become ever more subject to estrangement. A culture which increasingly employs feeling in the service of business, she argues, places a correspondingly high value on the spontaneous and the natural. And traditionally the management of feeling—what Hochschild calls "emotion management"—"has been better understood and more often used by women as one of the offerings they trade for economic support."[1] *Dombey*'s great subject is obviously the relationship between father and daughter, ending in Dombey's discovery of what everyone else discovered long ago: that "Dombey and

---

1. Arlie Russell Hochschild, *The Managed Heart: Commercialization of Human Feeling* (Berkeley and Los Angeles: University of California Press, 1983), pp. 20 and 22. Subsequent references in text.

Son [is] a Daughter after all" (298). But Florence's victory is essentially a victory of emotion over convention, of the natural over the artificial, and of private life over public life, as the novel links and structures these categories. *Dombey and Son* and its omniscient narration may be seen as doing the cultural work which both maintains and reproduces the natural, the emotions, and the inner life as centers of value in a world in which feeling is, to use Hochschild's term, increasingly "instrumental."[2] Pitting private against public, interior against exterior, the "world within" against the "world without," and Florence against Dombey, *Dombey and Son* enforces the essentiality and the irreducibility of what it constructs as the private, the interior, the "natural"—what Richard Sennett has called "identity composed of materials from within."[3] In doing so, the novel contributes to the emptying out of public life which is Sennett's concern, while assuring its readers that authentic feeling exists and can survive intact in a world of business.

Discussing such pseudosciences as phrenology and physiognomy, Sennett suggests that the Victorians both believed and feared that everything about them was visible.

> [I]n the high Victorian era people believed their clothes and their speech disclosed their personalities; they feared that these signs were equally beyond their power to mold, but would instead be manifest to others in involuntary tricks of speech, body gesture, or even how they adorned themselves. (25)

What follows, Sennett argues, is a loss of belief in individual ability to control the way appearances are interpreted and the development of an anxiety about "giving [oneself] away." As I have already suggested, *Dombey's* omniscience reflects what must have been characteristic of nineteenth-century life, given

2. My argument here might seem to resemble Steven Marcus's discussion of the "death of feeling" in *Dickens: From Pickwick to Dombey*, except that, as I see it, representing feeling as "dead" in one sphere brings it to life in another.

3. Richard Sennett, *The Fall of Public Man* (New York: Vintage, 1978), p. 9. Subsequent references in text.

a belief in physiognomy and the ability of appearances to convey essential truths: namely, the epistemological power that readers, spectators, or narrators have—or imagine they have—over participants. Sennett's focus on the anxiety such "reading" arouses is especially appropriate for a consideration of Dickens's sketches and novels, which are interested not only in the reading of surface marks, but also in a character's inability to control his or her self-representation. Moments at which a narrator points out such failures serve two purposes. They establish the existence of a "natural" self, and in doing so they secure the novel's omniscience, which perceives—and by perceiving validates—that self. For just as Dickens's work sets up an opposition between public and private worlds, so too does it articulate one between a "true" inner self and a "false," because publicly oriented, outer self that would manage "true" character, keeping it imprisoned. True character reveals itself in the incompleteness of a character's control over his or her appearance, and the narrator establishes his power over his characters, just as the characters do over one another, by noting these lapses of control. Thus, purporting to see through to true character, this narrative technique establishes its own truth value. The narrator sets himself up as an eye that sees beyond what is presented for public consumption.

For Sennett, the only sure defense against vulnerability to the reading of others, the only way to maintain a boundary between the self and the public world, is "to try to keep oneself from feeling, to have no feelings to show" (26). From this perspective, Dombey's characteristic behavior may be regarded as a response to the insistently public world *Dombey and Son* depicts, one in which the individual has no privacy other than what he can develop by having nothing to reveal. Dombey's desire not to express feeling might thus be considered a "natural" result of the publicity of his age: in such a world, that is, it would be "natural to be unnatural" (*Dombey*, 737).

But Dombey, the narrator assures us, does feel, and despite his attempts to hide it his feeling reveals itself. "[H]e cannot hide those rebel traces of it, which escape in hollow eyes and cheeks, a haggard forehead, and a moody, brooding air. Impenetrable as before . . . he is humbled, or those marks would not be there" (808–9). The novel stages a competition between world without and world within, a competition the latter has already won both because the narrator pursues Dombey when he hides (exposing, as if to spite him, what he would not have others know) and because the relationship between inner self and outer is represented as that of prisoner to prison, the inner self always trying to escape and always succeeding in doing so. Characters' attempts at managing their feelings thus give way before the power and intensity of their inner, "natural" selves, those selves whose presence the narrator insistently confirms merely by revealing what speaks for itself ("or those marks would not be there").

But what exactly is it that is being confirmed, that speaks for itself? Hochschild distinguishes between two kinds of emotion management, based on two schools of acting: "surface" acting, which involves the manipulation of appearance, and "deep" or "method" acting, which concentrates on the engendering of feeling. In general terms, the first involves the cultivation of the appearance of feeling; the second, of feeling itself.[4] *Dombey* stages, as I have said, the victory of the "natural" self. But this victory, as we shall see, requires management of a particular kind: it requires deep rather than surface acting.

Omniscience shows what any keen-eyed observer might see—what individuals themselves "give away." But most characteristically it shows what no one sees, what characters keep to themselves or what no one cares to see. By emphasizing what "no one knows," *Dombey*'s narration signals the importance of what characters do when they are alone, establishing the value of privacy for the revelation of true character. And, in a displacement of privacy from the external to the internal sphere, as well as in an evasion of its own publicizing activity, the novel establishes what is essential to our evalua-

4. See Hochschild on "deep" or "method" acting, pp. 37–48 and passim.

tion of *Dombey*'s characters. The crucial issue is not *whether* characters are being watched—for, indeed, they are all being watched. Rather, it is their sensitivity to public attention, whether they know or care that they are being watched— whether, that is, they are creatures shaped by and responsive to the publicity that characterizes their age, or whether they have stubbornly, like Captain Cuttle, remained "old fashioned." Alerting us to the importance of what goes on when no one is watching, *Dombey and Son* valorizes characters— Florence above all—whose primary attribute is their inattention to the public world, characters who prefer to be alone, with whom we spend long periods in private, and who, even in public, are incapable of "surface" acting. Linking the values of privacy and the natural, Dickens thus manages the unmanaged heart, constructing the natural and the private in opposition to the unnatural and the public, establishing an emotional system in which characters are valued to the extent that they are able to ignore the public world.[5] *Dombey and Son* depicts an unnatural world which prizes those who "act naturally."

Emphasizing the importance of what no one knows, *Dombey* makes itself significant in its possession of, and interest in, information that—it claims—does not circulate. Such is the force of its recurring critique of what the "Papers" say, their tendency to "work" information "up in print, in a most surprising manner" (835–36). (Indeed, given that *Dombey* follows upon Dickens's foray into the newspaper business as the editor of the *Daily News,* we can see in this contrast his preference for the secrets of the heart which are the novel's business over the kind of news the papers report.) At the same time, by claiming the possession of knowledge no one knows, the novel places itself in a larger context within which what is valued appears to exist outside, and untouched by, the marketplace. This is the essence of Florence's value, as well as of the contrast between Edith, who is unnaturally made conscious of her status as a marketable commodity, and Florence,

5. For "emotional system," see Hochschild, *The Managed Heart,* p. 12.

whose naturalness results from her having been left—through neglect—to her "natural heart." Florence, who for Dombey is "base coin," appears to escape the laws of the marketplace, including those laws which govern the exchange of women, and embodies instead the values that Dickens poses as an alternative to those of the marketplace, both in her person and in the qualities she represents throughout the novel.[6]

For Florence's value inheres in her performance of actions and expression of feelings that have no exchange value within the novel: she is "possessed of so much affection that no one seemed to care to have" (81). It is not that her feelings aren't powerful. On the contrary, her possession of Paul's and Edith's affection places her in direct rivalry with Dombey. Her feelings are instrumental, her apparent non-management of feeling, as we shall see, a way of managing herself and others.[7] But her feelings importantly *appear* non-instrumental because, though Dombey rejects her, Florence "never changes": she gives even though she receives nothing in return. This is the force of what she does that no one sees; these scenes are in fact instrumental less for Florence than for us. Her love has power for the reader because it appears useless, and therefore pure; it finds its value not primarily, or not first, within the novel, but outside it, in the act of exchange that is reading. Florence's feelings circulate among us. She may be "base coin" for Dombey, but in her own currency—feeling—she is a pearl of great price. Her emotions, which within the novel provide a refuge from the marketplace, are precisely what give her value in the marketplace in which the novel circulates.

The novel's valorization of non-instrumental feeling can be linked to the emotions the novel evokes. *Dombey* has been

6. Robert Clark discusses Florence's relation to the "exchange of women" argument in "Riddling the Family Firm: The Sexual Economy in *Dombey and Son*," *ELH* 51 (1984): 69–84.

7. On the power of Florence's feelings, see Nina Auerbach, "Dickens and Dombey: A Daughter After All," in *Dickens Studies Annual* 5 (1976): 95–105; Louise Yelin, "Strategies for Survival: Florence and Edith in *Dombey and Son*," *Victorian Studies* 22 (1979): 297–319; and Julian Moynahan, "Dealings with the Firm of Dombey and Son: Firmness vs. Wetness," in Gross and Pearson, eds., *Dickens and the Twentieth Century*, pp. 121–31.

particularly prized for the feeling it arouses in readers. Indeed, the death of Paul was a deliberate attempt on Dickens's part to recreate the pathos he had achieved with the death of Little Nell.[8] For the reader, the novel (and not only *Dombey and Son*) becomes a place to experience what is perceived as noninstrumental feeling: feeling which represents an alternative to the emotional management performed elsewhere. Hochschild's "emotional labor" thus has its counterpart in emotional recreation of the type *Dombey* and other Victorian novels provide, in the imagining of a place—the novel—where the "inner life" can exist free of the constraints it encounters in public. The novel is thus most instrumental in its construction of a world within—one that, in its fantasmatic nature, it is the omniscient narrator's privilege to oversee.

Even as the novel constructs a world of feeling within each individual, it also forges another inner world, one that its culture imagined as its primary refuge from the public world and the marketplace: the family. Nancy Armstrong argues that the novel plays a crucial role in what she calls government through the family, pointing out that fiction "helped to formulate the ordered space we call the household . . . and used it as the context for representing normal behavior."[9] The novel, Armstrong writes, naturalizes cultural and political values by "presuming to discover what was only natural in the self" (9). Armstrong traces a movement in the mid-nineteenth century from government through force to government by means of the use of strategies of surveillance centering on educational institutions and the family—a movement *Dombey* replicates in its replacement of Dombey's repressive rule with a familial world centered on Florence, the novel's chief agent of surveillance from within. And what the household accomplishes through surveillance, the novel accomplishes by enabling its

---

8. See, for example, pt. I, ch. 1 ("Origins and Reception") in Alan Shelston, ed., *"Dombey and Son" and "Little Dorrit": A Casebook* (London: Macmillan, 1985), especially comments by Macaulay and Jeffrey, p. 32.

9. Nancy Armstrong, *Desire and Domestic Fiction* (New York: Oxford University Press, 1987), introduction and pp. 23–24. Subsequent references in text.

readers to see through the rooftop, becoming, Asmodeus-like, secret observers of family life.

Armstrong argues that though the household, as a female domain, might appear to exist outside political life, in its disciplinary and educational work and its inculcation of "civilizing" values, it plays a crucial political role. *Dombey* naturalizes the family by presenting it as endangered and disrupted by the external force of business, enacted in Dombey's fundamental confusion of firm and family—a confusion which results in his dislike for his daughter and his too-great reliance on Carker. In order to locate the sources of its tensions outside the family, that is, the novel must make them the result of desires it terms alien or unnatural even to their owner. The unnatural, then, is defined as whatever fails to support the idea of family that the novel itself constructs. Only when Dombey gives way to the "sense of injustice" that, Dickens claims, is "within him, all along" (1867 Preface) can he and his family recover their "natural" affection for one arother.

Dombey divides its characters into good and bad according to their desire for privacy or publicity. Linking goodness with privacy, the novel contrasts those characters who act with at least one eye on the effects of their actions with those who seek no power or recognition. The novel's good characters keep themselves hidden, letting their deeds go unrewarded ("one has no business to take credit for good intentions," says Morfin [842]); its evil characters attempt to impose their vision on the world, destroying the difference between themselves and the world. Little Paul keeps "his character to himself" (234); Mr. Carker the Junior seeks to remain "unquestioned and unnoticed" (247). By contrast, Carker the Manager is all effect. Above all a crafter of his own public image, what he chiefly manages are feelings, and he manipulates those of others by appearing to manipulate his own.[10] His manner toward Dombey is "deeply conceived and perfectly expressed" (239), and under his "skillful culture" Dombey grows increas-

---

10. The word "carker" means "harass." Dickens uses the term to describe the state of mind of Blimber's students: "The young gentlemen were prematurely full of carking anxieties" (208).

ingly angry at Florence (443). Typically, Carker keeps his "true" self hidden, never betraying "his own hand" (372)—a hand revealed to the reader, however, who knows that "alone in his own room he shows his teeth all day" (311). Dickens's omniscience insists on the difference between the public and the private spheres that it happily transgresses, earning our allegiance by showing us what characters are truly like, which means showing us what they are like when they think no one sees them.

> As Mr. Dombey dropped his eyes, and adjusted his neck-cloth again, the smiling face of Mr. Carker the Manager became in a moment, and without any stage of transition, transformed into a most intent and frowning face, scanning his closely, and with an ugly sneer. As Mr. Dombey raised his eyes, it changed back, no less quickly, to its old expression, and showed him every gum of which it stood possessed. (442)

Though it is characteristic of Carker to hide "beneath his manner" (690), the narrator makes a point of showing us his failure to control himself. Managing his manner, but not his emotions, Carker cannot keep his "true" self from emerging. "Wolf's face that it was then, with even the hot tongue revealing itself through the stretched mouth, as the eyes encountered Mr. Dombey's!" (442).[11]

But while Carker's lack of control signifies weakness, Florence's bespeaks naturalness: Florence cannot dissimulate. When she is under surveillance, called upon to play with Paul under her father's eye, her manner is "forced and embarrassed" (86). Throughout long sections of the novel we watch as she suffers, silent and alone, in Dombey's house. During much of this time, she herself observes the private domestic scenes that take place in the window of the house across the way, scenes of "rosy children" who possess their father's love. This watching, the narrator tells us, is her "secret," as is her other activity: the vigil she maintains outside her father's door.

11. Indeed, Carker's manipulativeness, his craftiness and feline "softness" are so impressed upon us that it is difficult to believe he does not "betray his hand" to other characters. His presentation resembles that of stage villainy, in which convention demands that other characters simply do not see what is made unmistakably clear to the audience.

> When no one in the house was stirring, and the lights were all
> extinguished, she would softly leave her own room, and with
> noiseless feet descend the staircase, and approach her father's
> door. Against it, scarcely breathing, she would rest her face
> and head, and press her lips, in the yearning of her love. . . .
>   No one knew it. No one thought of it. (320)

And again:

> It would have been a strange sight, to see her now, stealing
> lightly down the stairs through the thick gloom, and stopping
> at it [his door] with a beating heart, and blinded eyes, and hair
> that fell down loosely and unthought of; and touching it out-
> side with her wet cheek. But the night covered it, and no one
> knew. (327)

Later, with Dombey gone, Florence wanders among the
gloomy furniture in the silent house, "unsuspected and un-
aided" (398). "Still no one knew" (396). Florence does what
she does supremely indifferent to matters of appearance, under cover of darkness, her hair "unthought of," her single-
mindedness and sincerity attested not just by the simple fact
that she "never changes"—that her private actions reinforce
her public ones—but by the fact that she does so much, and
we see her do so much, in private. The point—"still no one
knew"—could hardly be stressed more. What Florence does
counts because she does it when, and even though—and,
with respect to the way the novel constructs her naturalness,
because—no one knows about it.

   If the naturalness of Florence's feelings is affirmed by her
extensive private indulgence in them, it is reinforced by what
happens when she does have an audience. For it is important
to the representation of Florence's "natural" self that she cannot manipulate her manner; she cannot keep her private feelings from spilling over into public life. Further, the novel
implies, natural feeling proves its naturalness by its refusal to
be controlled; if temporarily mastered, it will not remain so.
True feeling appears to be true because it cannot respect the
boundary between public and private spheres; in Dickens's
rhetoric, it has a will of its own and cannot be commanded. "It
was a natural emotion, not to be suppressed; and it would
make its way even between the fingers of the hand with which

she covered up her face. The overcharged and heavy-laden breast must sometimes have that vent, or the poor wounded solitary heart within it would have fluttered like a bird with broken wings, and sunk down in the dust" (316). It is essential to the appearance of "natural" emotion that it disregard conventions of time and place; melodramatically, it appears when it must. Hochschild defines "emotional management" as an "indication of will" involving feeling (13). In contrast to those managers of feeling Chick and Tox, Florence, it seems, cannot "make an effort."

> ". . . it is our duty to submit."
> "I will try, dear aunt, I do try," answered Florence, sobbing. (313)

> "Edith," said Mr. Dombey, "this is my daughter Florence. Florence, this lady will soon be your Mama."
> Florence started, and looked up at the beautiful face in a conflict of emotions, among which the tears that name awakened, struggled for a moment with surprise, interest, admiration, and an indefinable sort of fear. Then she cried out, "Oh, Papa, may you be happy! may you be very, very happy all your life!" and then fell weeping on the lady's bosom.
> There was a short silence. (486)

The natural appears to be natural because it is naturally awkward, carefully structured to clash with the conventions that govern others' behavior. Indifferent to the expectations of others, it opposes behavior which exists purely to evoke a response in others, behavior which is pure calculation.

> Mr. Dombey leaned back in his chair, instead of bending over the papers that were laid before him, and looked the Manager steadily in the face. The Manager, with his eyelids slightly raised, affected to be glancing at his figures, and to await the leisure of his principal. He showed that he affected this, as if from great delicacy. (443)

Carker's "skillful culture," the management of Dombey's emotions through the management of his own manner, is work of some complexity, uncovering levels of emotional duplicity as it "shows" what it "affects."

Almost every character in the novel is presented as being in a state of inward struggle, willing, or failing to will, feeling.

Unable to hide her true feeling for Dombey, Edith sells herself, or lets herself be sold. Just as Dombey's face is "marked" and Florence's feelings force their way through her fingers, so too does Edith's body speak for her: her beauty appears "against her will" (367). Such struggle, valued as an indication of the presence of natural feeling, is juxtaposed to the easy manipulation of the appearance of feeling, as when Mrs. Skewton embraces Florence, who had "certainly never undergone so much embracing, and perhaps had never been, unconsciously, so useful in her life" (509). Though the narrator tells us that "habit" may cause the unnatural to become natural, it never quite does for many of *Dombey*'s characters, whose natural feeling is in a constant state of rebellion against the unnatural uses to which it is put.

As its critics have remarked, *Dombey and Son* is an especially melodramatic novel, containing a number of scenes in which behavior seems to transgress conventional boundaries, as, for example, the scene in which Edith announces to Dombey her desire for a separation in the presence of Florence and Carker. To some extent, "melodrama" describes the perception that we are witnessing private material—a perception enhanced here by Dombey's insistence that Carker and Florence remain in the room as a means of humiliating his wife. In staging this scene Dombey deliberately blurs the boundary between his business world and his private life. As he does so, the novel outrages what it defines as "natural," as "sense": the reader's "sense" of privacy. The presence of an audience encourages the apprehension that we have unintentionally stumbled into a family conflict, that we witness the private "by accident." At the same time, it makes the site of such conflict one of intense feeling and interest. Like Carker—"Carker listened, with his eyes cast down" (746)—we may avert our eyes, but we are no less attentive.[12]

Peter Brooks uses the term "melodrama" to describe the rep-

---

12. See Yelin, "Strategies for Survival"; and William F. Axton, *Circle of Fire: Dickens' Vision and Style and the Popular Victorian Theater* (Lexington: University of Kentucky Press, 1966), on Dickens's use of melodrama.

resentation of a "victory over repression," of actions which, like dreams, erase distinctions between desire and action, and scenes which permit the saying of the unsayable.[13] For Brooks, such scenes reassure audiences and readers because they resolve complex emotional situations into an absolute difference between good and evil. When Dombey strikes Florence, however, or when Edith speaks the unspeakable to Dombey or tears his jewels from her breast ("Did you think that I loved you? Did you know that I did not? Did you ever care, Man! for my heart, or propose to yourself to win the worthless thing?" [654]), the novel stages a battle in which one character's authentic feeling struggles against another's desire to preserve appearances ("Do you know who I am, Madam? Do you know what I represent?" [749]). (Even while making a point of his desire to preserve appearances, however, Dombey cannot but reveal the scandal of this relationship to Carker and Florence, and, in contrast to Carker, he appears ineffectual here in his inability to control knowledge about himself.) But what appears excessive or melodramatic in these demonstrations, as in Florence's effusions of feeling, is a response to a cultural need to make natural feeling visible because feeling in the main has been put in the service of the unnatural, given over to management, becoming, like Carker's, deformed by the requirements of public representation.

It is evidence of Florence's naturalness that, like Captain Cuttle, she cannot adapt to the modern world and has no place in it.[14] Her character is interior both in the sense that we see her from the inside (that is, we read her thoughts) and that she seems to belong indoors. Dickens emphasizes her old-fashionedness and her interiority by twice thrusting her suddenly and unexpectedly into the public sphere, in what almost seems like an irruption of privacy into that sphere: once, when she is lost by Susan Nipper in the City, and a second time, after

13. See Brooks, *The Melodramatic Imagination*, chs. 1 and 2.
14. Of Florence and Captain Cuttle, Dickens writes: "[I]n simple innocence of the world's ways and the world's perplexities and dangers, they were nearly on a level" (776).

Dombey strikes her, when she takes flight there, the second instance in some ways recapitulating the first.

> Where to go? Still somewhere, anywhere! still going on; but where! She thought of the only other time she had been lost in the wild wilderness of London—though not lost as now—and went that way. To the home of Walter's Uncle. . . . The roar soon grew more loud, the passengers more numerous, the shops more busy, until she was carried onward in a stream of life setting that way, and flowing, indifferently, past marts and mansions, prisons, churches, market-places, wealth, poverty, good, and evil. . . . At length the quarters of the little Midshipman arose in view. (759)

Florence's bewilderment, her incapacity to understand where she is except insofar as it leads to the Midshipman's, as well as Dickens's emphasis on the "indifference" and impersonality of the "stream of life" that surrounds her, all serve to emphasize her essential interiority. And in both instances, the Midshipman's—the antipodes of Dombey and Son, the shop from which nothing is ever sold—becomes her refuge, its reminders of Walter, lost on the high seas, pointing to the advisability of never going outdoors.

Throughout the novel, the natural is constructed in contrast with and opposition to the unnatural: what is forced, imposed from without, or requires "making an effort." "Breeding" and "nature" are everywhere opposed. Morfin takes leave of Harriet "with such a happy mixture of unconstrained respect and unaffected interest, as no breeding could have taught" (562). "Forcing" is explored in the Blimber's Academy scenes, in Mrs. Skewton's perversion of Edith's "natural heart," in Mrs. Skewton's own travesties of nature—and, primarily, in Dombey's desire to hurry Paul through his childhood as quickly as possible. "It being a part of Mrs. Pipchin's system not to encourage a child's mind to develop and expand itself like a young flower, but to open it by force like an oyster . . ." (163); "Doctor Blimber's establishment was a great hothouse, in which there was a forcing apparatus constantly at work. . . . Nature was of no consequence at all" (206). What is natural is what is left to grow in its own direction, unwilled and un-

forced. Left on its own, the novel insists, the heart will naturally form familial affections: "She yearned towards him, and
yet shrunk from his approach. Unnatural emotion in a child,
innocent of wrong! Unnatural the hand that had directed the
sharp plough, which furrowed up her gentle nature for the
sowing of its seeds!" (585). And those affections will, ultimately, find expression. Even Carker (we are told) in his last
moments "may" have a touch of familial feeling: "If ever he
remembered sister or brother with a touch of tenderness and
remorse, who shall say it was not then?" (874).

Dombey's marital difficulties and the ruin of the firm only
heighten the difference between "the world," which makes
use of Dombey's misfortune in various ways, and those who
respond to the disaster by remaining loyal to Dombey and
doing good in secret—those who, like Florence, stubbornly
insist upon an idea of family against all indications to the
contrary, treating Dombey and Son as a family rather than a
firm. The disaster creates publicity and celebrity: "The world
was very busy . . . and had a deal to say" (908). Mr. Perch becomes famous over the bankruptcy, as he did over the elope-
ment. The clerks, who have no particular attachment to Dombey, disperse. Only Morfin continues to work on clearing up
Dombey's affairs, retiring to his home at night to confide his
cares to his violoncello. Harriet Carker's plan to channel some
of her and her brother's newly acquired money to Dombey
must be implemented "quietly and secretly" (915). Most strikingly, perhaps, the novel contrasts those who consider their
employment by both family and firm as mere employment
with those who regard it as a familial attachment. The ruin
of the firm and the household creates a kind of community
among the servants. The strife between Dombey and Edith
gives them a "good subject for a rallying point" (743) and the
bankruptcy provides them with cause for feasting. But in
Morfin and in Harriet—as in the relationship between Susan
Nipper and Florence—the novel celebrates a kind of feudal
bond between servants and master which has no actual connection with the way the firm of Dombey and Son operates,
and which, fittingly, has no point or purpose until the firm's

demise. Dombey's business methods are superseded by, and found to be inferior to, work performed out of love or loyalty, work which asks no recognition.

In its efforts to separate the natural from the unnatural, family from business, and good characters from bad ones, *Dombey and Son* also separates good watching from bad. The novel's omniscience attempts to naturalize itself by thematizing the secret observation of others. Dombey keeps Richards under surveillance; Carker watches everyone and employs Rob the Grinder as his spy; Good Mrs. Brown warns Florence that "there would be potent eyes and ears in her employment cognizant of all she did" (131). The novel's separation of good from bad watching (or the good spirit from the lame demon, as the difference is later formulated) represents an attempt to resolve the ambivalence that attends covert observation and to associate itself with the former rather than the latter. Any "secret intelligence" gained by Morfin, for example, is used for good, its secrecy a result of his desire not to "take credit for good intentions" (842). But while Carker, Dombey's "confidential agent" in business and personal affairs, resembles other narratorial personae in Dickens's work (such as Boz and John Harmon) in his ability to move between these realms, that ability is here defined as sinister. Just as Master Humphrey disappeared, scapegoating Quilp as that novel's intrusive spy, so too does *Dombey's* narration attempt to distance itself from a figure it disturbingly resembles. And yet Carker, with his powers of observation and ability to move between public and private life, is inescapably linked to the narrator. It is chiefly through him, for instance, that we register the truth of Edith's feeling about Dombey:

> All this time, Edith never raised her eyes, unless to glance towards her mother. . . . But as Carker ceased, she looked at Mr. Dombey for a moment. For a moment only; but with a transient gleam of scornful wonder on her face, not lost on one observer, who was smiling round the board. (463)

The momentary escape of Edith's true feeling is "not lost"— but neither is Carker's observation of it. Conscious as he is, there is unseen intelligence above and beyond him, and it is by means of this intelligence that the novel's narration anxiously attempts to separate itself from him, while continuing to "employ" him. Though we are told that he saw Edith "in his mind, exactly as she was" (735), Carker turns out, of course, to be wrong. In language which returns in *Bleak House*, and using a method later to appear in *Our Mutual Friend*, Dickens demonstrates the "springing of his [Carker's] mine upon himself" (735), revealing that, as far as Edith is concerned, Carker mistakes the projection of his own desire for truth.

While the narration attempts to separate itself from Carker's observations, however, it endorses Florence's. One of the primary ways in which *Dombey and Son* valorizes the private is by aligning itself, and consequently the reader, with Florence. Though she stands for the private and the domestic, she is (next to Carker) the novel's most penetrating observer. Seeing with Florence, narrator and readers—unlike "the world" which pursues Dombey, and unlike the merely curious stranger—see for the sake of the private. It is Florence's vision, finally, that the novel naturalizes, and that naturalizes Dombey and Son—family, firm, and novel.

Florence, little Paul notices, is "always watching": "You are always watching me, Floy. Let me watch *you*, now!" (293). Dombey feels that she has "eyes that read his soul" (355) and that "she watched and distrusted him. As if she held the clue to something secret in his breast . . ." (84). She is watching when we first encounter her; her initial observation of Dombey, at the time of his wife's death, makes him uneasy about her. And it is through Florence that the narrator seems to comment on his own activity, raising the question of the moral status of unseen observation at the moment when she sees a "dark shape" issuing from her home, "the figure of a man coming down some few stairs opposite. . . . It was Mr. Carker coming down alone. . . . Her invincible repugnance to this man, and perhaps the stealthy act of watching anyone, which, even under such innocent circumstances, is in a manner guilty and oppressive, made Florence shake from head to foot" (752). Aligned with Florence, the reader is placed in the same paradoxical position he or she is in when learning what "no one knows," the position of valuing the private while learning—as if unwittingly "even under such innocent circumstances"—the secrets of others. Above all, we become Florence's allies in the desire to uncover the individual "world within" for the familial "world within": to break down Dombey's rigid, public facade, uncovering his private, feeling self, and to make him learn, in a way he will never forget, the value of the family, of feeling, of domestic life.

Rather than simply revealing what exists, Florence's watching has a certain shaping power. Discussing triangular structures of desire in the novel, Diane Sadoff has argued that Florence uses Dombey to mediate her desire, seeing him as her rival for the love of others.[15] Florence's watching reveals her repressed anger against Dombey. We might also say that it expresses a kind of vehemence against Paul: that she watches him to death. That suspicion is augmented by her fantasy of her life had she been a "favourite child."

> She imagined so often what her life would have been if her father could have loved her and she had been a favourite child, that sometimes, for the moment, she almost believed it was so, and, borne on by the current of that pensive fiction, seemed to remember how they had watched her brother in the grave together; how they had freely shared his heart between them; how they were united in the dear remembrance of him. (396)

Alone, Florence can have, or imagine that she will have, the father she does not possess in reality, and she can have him because, as this cannibalistic image suggests, both now possess Paul. But the image of standing with her father over Paul's grave expresses not just a desire to have her father to herself, but also a desire for revenge; her fantasies about her own death convey the same feeling ("Yes, she thought if she were dying, he would relent" [426]). And when, after Dombey's accident, Florence approaches the sickbed where he lies sleep-

---

15. Diane Sadoff, *Monsters of Affection* (Baltimore: Johns Hopkins University Press, 1982), pp. 60–62.

ing, her thoughts about his unconsciousness of her mingle with her never-acknowledged fantasies of his death.

> As she looked upon it now, she saw it, for the first time, free from the cloud that had darkened her childhood. . . . There was no change upon his face; and as she watched it, awfully, its motionless repose recalled the faces that were gone. So they looked, so would he; so she, his weeping child, who should say when! so all the world of love and hatred and indifference around them! (698)

Dombey sleeping resembles Dombey dead. In either state, the disturbing reflection of Florence is absent from his face. (But it is also oddly present: in "not changing," Dombey resembles Florence.) The idea of Dombey's death comes as a relief to her, presenting an image of the father she cannot have while he is alive and aware of her.

For, spontaneous and natural as she appears to be, Florence's fantasies are in fact the novel's most powerful manifestation of emotional management, of willing feeling. The chapter entitled "The Study of a Loving Heart" demonstrates that, in order to be "loving" in the face of continual rejection, the heart needs to be disciplined: "she must be careful in no thoughtless word, or look, or burst of feeling awakened by any chance circumstance, to complain against him" (423). Florence's solitude—or Dombey's unconsciousness—enables her to imagine him as she wants him, and that imagining requires an effort. Indeed, the presence of others interferes with it; the world is too full of references to unkind fathers (423). And since Florence deliberately focuses on "her idea of a father" (51), her darkest hour comes after Dombey strikes her, when he "murders," as she puts it, "the last lingering natural aspect in which she had cherished him through so much" (779). Her subsequent fear of seeing her image in the mirror—"the sight of the darkening mark upon her bosom made her afraid of herself, as if she bore about her something wicked" (779)—emerges from the desire not to see the bad father she could not help but see if she looked, the evidence for which she now (literally) bears. By refusing to look, she avoids seeing Dombey as he is, a sight which would interfere with her desire to imagine him as she desires him to be. And what, after this, she "comes to love" when she thinks of her father is an image which suggests that he has, in fact, died. He becomes to her "a dear remembrance," one with "something of the softened sadness with which she remembered little Paul" (739).

For Dickens, as the phrase "the last lingering natural aspect" signals, Florence's fantasizing represents not management but a clinging to nature in the face of the unnatural. What she envisions *is*, in the novel's terms, Dombey's natural self. Seeing with Florence thus means more than seeing through her eyes: it means perceiving the truth of what she sees. The novel affirms not the fantasmatic nature of her vision, but the unreality, the unnaturalness, of what does not conform to it. Those who respond to Dombey's actual behavior—Edith and Carker—are ruined, it seems, because they do so. Almost unbelievably, when the mist falls from Dombey's eyes and he sees Florence's "true" self (935), the novel seems to endorse his perception that little Paul, Edith, and Carker are equal, and equally disloyal, in their changeableness to Dombey. Even little Paul's death, from this point of view, becomes a betrayal: "His boy had faded into dust, his proud wife had sunk into a polluted creature, his flatterer and friend had been transformed into the worst of villains . . . she alone had turned the same mild gentle look upon him always" (935). And it is Florence's constancy that Dombey finally "knows," as the "unnatural" part of him "crumbles."

> He knew, now, what he had done. He knew, now, that he had called down that upon his head, which bowed it lower than the heaviest stroke of fortune. He knew, now, what it was to be rejected and deserted. (935)
>
> Strong mental agitation and disturbance was no novelty to him, even before his late sufferings. It never is, to obstinate and sullen natures; for they struggle hard to be such. Ground, long undermined, will often fall down in a moment; what was undermined here in so many ways, weakened, and crumbled, little by little, as the hand moved on the dial. (938)

The effort of maintaining the unnatural self is presented as management. This effort over, the ever-present natural self can emerge. And, as the scene has it, Florence causes no change in Dombey; the sameness of her look merely evokes a response from the natural self that has been within him all along. Knowledge of Florence—of her true self—is for Dombey the same, in the novel's terms, as knowledge of his natural self.

When Carker's perceptions of Edith turn out to be mistaken, he suffers severely. But though Florence shapes her perceptions of Dombey deliberately so as *not* to see him as he is, the novel confirms "her idea of a father." Why? Carker and Florence in fact represent two examples of management, alternative projections of the narrator's own enterprise: Carker is an example of "How Not To Do It"; Florence, exactly the opposite.[16] Carker is both too great and too little a manager. Though he is said never to betray his hand, his overt desire for control and deliberate manipulations of others prove his undoing. Excellent as he is at the art of dissimulation, it is exactly because he dissimulates that his desire for power can become visible and therefore subject to manipulation. Carker is too little a manager, that is, because he manipulates only his surface, managing not feelings but only their appearance—and, despite the depth of his knowledge of others, allowing himself to be deceived by his belief in his power over them.[17]

Florence, on the other hand, concentrates her powers of management on shaping her feelings, on disciplining herself. Her management consists of holding to her "good purpose," attempting to keep all thoughts of cruelty and unnaturalness from being associated with fathers, and concentrating on making her father aware of her love for him.

> He did not know how much she loved him. However long the time in coming, she must try to bring that knowledge to her father's heart one day or other. Meantime she must be careful in no thoughtless word, or look, or burst of feeling awakened

16. The management styles of Florence and Carker are juxtaposed in the monthly installment made up of chapters 20–25.

17. I cannot refrain from quoting a phrase from Wayne Booth here—who argues that omniscience which doesn't display itself is nevertheless omniscience. It is in fact, Booth says, "omniscience with teeth in it": *The Rhetoric of Fiction*, 2d ed. (Chicago: University of Chicago Press, 1983), p. 161.

by any chance circumstance, to complain against him, or to
give occcasion for these whispers to his prejudice. (423)

Dombey and Son, in other words, prefers genuine emotional
management to what only appears to be emotional management: it prefers "deep" to surface acting. And Dickens uses
Florence's emotional management to manage the entire novel.

Critics discussing Florence's influence on Dombey falter in
describing the exact form this influence takes. She has what
Louise Yelin calls a "commanding submissiveness," but precisely how her submissiveness commands is difficult to pin-
point.[18] Nina Auerbach writes that the manner in which she
influences Dombey is "ungraspable by definition."[19] Nor is it
easy to separate the effect her "submissiveness" has on Dombey from its effect on the reader, for Florence's fantasies circulate mainly between herself and the reader. But Florence's
management is difficult to perceive precisely because, like the
narrator's, it does not appear as management. Her chief action
consists of "never changing"; concentrating her efforts on
herself, she behaves *as if* her desires *are* reality. Like Morfin,
and like Harriet Carker, Florence remains true to an ideal of
familial affection even when—in fact, especially when—it remains absent from her experience. Like a method actor, Florence gets what she wants by acting as if she already has it.
And the novel affirms the worthiness of, and eventually realizes, this ideal. For both Florence and the omniscient narrator,
then, the difference between desire and reality, or between
perception and *construction*, disappears. Where bad management—Carker or Dombey—must exercise control and attempt to subdue the world to its will, good management
appears not to control at all, but simply waits until others
become (as they inevitably must) their natural selves. Such
control operates from within rather than from without: it operates, that is, at the level of establishing the natural. As a
narratorial projection, then, Florence might be said to represent not a fantasy of omniscience as control, but one of omni-

18. Yelin, "Strategies for Survival," p. 301.
19. Auerbach, "Dickens and Dombey," p. 101.

science as *lack* of control. Naturalizing Florence's desires, the narration reveals as inevitable what Florence and the omniscient narrator have always "known"—because they affirmed it—to be so. Whereas Florence is all feeling, Dombey, of course, is all resistance to feeling. Dombey characteristically imagines himself as a witness to the emotions of others.

> The last time he had seen his slighted child, there had been in that sad embrace between her and her dying mother, what was at once a revelation and a reproach to him. Let him be as absorbed in the Son on whom he built such high hopes, he could not forget that closing scene. He could not forget that he had no part in it. That, at the bottom of its clear depths of tenderness and truth, lay those two figures clasped in each other's arms, while he stood on the bank above them, looking down—a mere spectator—not a sharer with them—quite shut out. (83)

Emotion creates a place from which Dombey feels excluded; or, we might say, Dombey positions himself so that he is excluded from emotional scenes. Such scenes recur between Florence and Fanny, Florence and Paul, Florence and Edith, with Dombey always the silent spectator. He perceives in these scenes emotion in which he cannot share, emotion which robs him of his property in Edith or in little Paul. But Dombey also imagines the emotions of others as a threat to him: anyone else's feeling for Paul undermines his hold on the boy. Thus while he experiences himself as shut out of emotional scenes, he also, as we have seen, repeatedly shuts himself up in order to experience emotion in private. Dombey's spectatorship suggests both vicarious participation and a need to distance himself from feeling. He invites Carker to become the mediator of his relations with Edith; he seeks someone to "interpose" between himself and Florence.

> It troubled him to think of this face of Florence.
> Because he felt any new compunction toward it? No. Because the feeling it awakened in him—of which he had had some old foreshadowing in older times—was full-formed now, and spoke out plainly, moving him too much, and threatening

to grow too strong for his composure. . . . More than once upon this journey, and now again as he stood pondering at this journey's end, tracing figures in the dust with his stick, the thought came into his mind, what was there he could interpose between himself and it? (356)

Whatever the specific cause of Dombey's "strong feeling," he distances himself from it, even seeking a wife, it seems, for precisely this reason. For although Edith's affectionate relationship with Florence disturbs him, it is exactly what he requires to maintain his anger against Florence.[20] Dombey's spectatorship at once expresses his power and reveals his weakness. Delegating Carker to humiliate Edith, he displays his strength while defending against the threatened loss of control that strong feeling evokes—in psychoanalytic terms, his gaze both evokes and elides the threat of castration.[21] The danger of becoming involved, of moving from observation to participation, is precisely what Carker's fate demonstrates. In his spectatorship and in his delegation of participation to Carker, however, Dombey reveals what is at stake in the observer's position.

In the scene in which he seeks something to "interpose" between himself and Florence, Dombey is troubled by Florence's face as it appears in his mind. Her face comes to stand for his defeat in the world, for little Paul's death—in general, for his inability to control Dombey and Son. For as "the face" appears in his mind, it also appears "abroad." He thinks of it in terms which resemble those of the passage (quoted on pp. 71–72) in which "the world" pursues him. "[T]he face was abroad, in the expression of defeat and persecution that seemed to encircle him like the air. . . . He saw her image in the blight and blackness all around him, not irradiating but deepening the gloom" (356). The appearance of Florence's face

20. The intention seems to be that Edith will interpose herself between Dombey and Florence, but Florence also becomes a wedge separating Edith from Dombey: "Florence would have risen when her father entered, and resigned her chair to him; but Edith openly put her hand upon her arm, and Mr. Dombey took an opposite place at the round table" (508).

21. See Sadoff, *Monsters of Affection*, p. 127.

both in Dombey's mind and "abroad" recalls the other passage's images of invasion: the world that is the "haunting
demon of his mind" (809), that he cannot keep out of his mind
or house, that anticipates him everywhere and is always busi-
est where he is not. Indeed, the face that "invades" Dombey's
mind reflects what seems to be for him a characteristic fear of
invasion. When he sees Toodles wearing a mourning band
which he deduces is for little Paul, Dombey imagines the
feelings of others as an assault on his privacy.

> So! from high to low, at home or abroad, from Florence in his
> great house to the coarse churl who was feeding the fire then
> smoking before them, everyone set up some claim or other to a
> share in his dead boy, and was a bidder against him! . . .
>   To think of this presumptuous raker among coals and ashes
> going on before there, with his sign of mourning! To think that
> he dared to enter, even by a common show like that, into the
> trial and disappointment of a proud gentleman's secret heart!
> To think that this lost child . . . should have let in such a herd
> to insult him with their knowledge of his defeated hopes, and
> their boasts of claiming community of feeling with himself, so
> far removed: if not of having crept into the place wherein he
> would have lorded it, alone! (353)

Dombey's fear of invasion is an extreme form of the bour-
geois desire for privacy. He wants too much privacy; he wants,
selfishly, to keep himself to himself. And he needs too much
privacy because he desires too much power: his fear of invasion is the perhaps inevitable result of imagining that "the
earth was made for Dombey and Son to trade in." Even as he
desires Dombey and Son to be "the world," he acknowledges
and therefore fears difference—for the presence of others signifies the existence of other worlds.

In the passage in which Dombey cannot escape "the
world," the narrator assures us that Dombey's sense of being
pursued is "not a phantom of his imagination" (809). The
narrator does so, it seems, because the passage too strongly
suggests paranoia, apparently depicting not what "the world"
is like but what it is like for Dombey. By assuring us of the
accuracy of Dombey's representation, however, the narrator

naturalizes Dombey's fear of the "world without." What seemed to belong to the character is asserted as a fact about the world.

The relationship between "world within" and "world without" has its stylistic analogue in those extended passages in which, employing what Dorrit Cohn calls "psycho-narration," the narrator reproduces a character's state of mind without abandoning third-person narration.[22] The most striking examples attempt to reproduce Paul's confusion during his illness and Carker's chaotic perceptions before his death. In these passages, while the character's consciousness reflects external events, we never lose sight of the narrator's mediating presence, nor do we lose the sense that "the world of the novel" differs from that character's immediate perception of it. But in the present case, the narrator and the events of the novel confirm Dombey's paranoia: his house *is* invaded by strangers. It is not Dombey's fancy that the world pursues and speaks of him everywhere; the arrival of Cousin Feenix and Major Bagstock proves it true. In other words, it is not that Dombey is paranoid. Everyone *is* talking about him. Because we cannot separate, in this instance, the narrator from Dombey—because this is not "psycho-narration" but simply narration—Dombey's desire to hide from the world "without" appears justified.

We may choose to believe, however, not that the world is like this, but that Dombey's paranoia is also the narrator's. In moments, that is, when the narrator endorses his characters' perceptions, the constructed nature of the narrator's world becomes evident. And the same merging, or slippage, between world without and world within occurs in the novel's naturalization of Florence's perceptions. In the days of his ruin, as he wanders his empty house alone, Dombey is insistently confronted with Florence's image: "she alone had turned the same mild gentle look upon him always" (935). And as he lets "the world" go from him, as he becomes "a

22. See Dorrit Cohn, *Transparent Minds* (Princeton: Princeton University Press, 1978), ch. 1.

spectral, haggard, wasted likeness of himself" (938), he is transformed into the father Florence desires, the father she and he can now see when they look in the mirror. "Suddenly it [his likeness] rose, with a terrible face, and that guilty hand grasping what was in its breast. Then it was arrested by a cry . . . and he only saw his own reflection in the glass, and at his knees, his daughter!" (939). As the "it"—his likeness—becomes "him," Dombey becomes "himself." In a kind of Lacanian mirror scene, when Dombey sees his reflection next to Florence's, the image he sees is mediated by her perception of him. From both within and without, the novel authorizes the self Dombey becomes after his fall as his "true" self; that is, it naturalizes Florence's projection. But the revelation appears to come from within and not from without. Dombey's internalization of Florence's image of himself is presented as his discovery of himself, the result of a natural development, caused by no unnatural will.

Dickens bends the novel to fit Florence's vision, so that it ends in a reconciliation founded on little Paul's memory. "We will teach our little child to love and honour you; and we will tell him, when he can understand, that you had a son of that name once, and that he died, and you were very sorry" (940). In the world according to Florence—a familial circle based on the remembrance of little Paul—the family, site of oedipal rivalry, is reconceived as a world all its own, a state of conflictlessness and undifferentiation, all rivals eliminated, the possessive love which engenders rivalry replaced by remembrance and sympathy. The family—or, more precisely, the community linked through remembrance of Paul and love of Florence—becomes a portable private space, a "community of feeling" (the phrase derives from the scene in which Dombey encounters Toodles).[23] Remembrance—shared sorrowful feeling—is offered as the alternative to possessiveness. Overcoming all other feelings, remembrance links the survivors in

---

23. The phrase "community of feeling" is used by Ian Milner: "The Dickens Drama: Mr. Dombey," in Nisbet and Nevius, eds., *Dickens Centennial Essays*, p. 155.

contemplation of the dead boy. The family is thus united by remembrance of Paul, but even more by devotion to Florence, a feeling even Mr. Toots, in his newly married state, affirms, as if to assure us that love of Florence can engender no rivalries. (According to him, Mrs. Toots, the former Susan Nipper, can only agree with her husband's opinion that Florence is "the most beautiful, the most amiable, the most angelic of her sex. What is her observation upon that? The perfection of sense. 'My dear, you're right. I think so too'" [973].) The novel thus enlarges the sphere of privacy, making it not selfish—the individual's solitary property—but familial, dissolving differences in the affirmation of shared feeling.

The novel ultimately replaces the public world of Dombey and Son with this world made of feeling, a private, self-sustaining, conflictless domestic world which cannot be violated by the public world because it does not acknowledge that world's existence. Once Walter has returned, Florence "never left her high rooms but to steal downstairs to wait for him when it was his time to come, or, sheltered by his proud, encircling arm, to bear him company to the door again, and sometimes peep into the street" (883). Yet when they marry, they can leave the house, not just for the streets but for the high seas, because Florence's love creates a world all its own, "a world to fly to, and to rest in, out of his [Walter's] one image" (884). In the end, Florence can "be happy anywhere" (885). As she and Walter walk to the church, they are "far removed from the world about them" (902), separated from the public sphere whose rapaciousness and irrelevance is represented in the destruction of Dombey's house and the misguided rumors the world "blabs" about him. Dombey's house has been revealed to be just that, a house—not the portable haven of domesticity, the home built out of feeling, which Florence recreates wherever she goes. Marriage creates a private space, distinct and safe from the inauthentic public space that surrounds it. The novel's lesson has been not only that Dombey and Son is "a Daughter, after all," but that Dombey and Son is a family, not a firm; or, if a firm, one reconceived in the image of the family.

But what is "the family"? The novel replaces one familial structure with another, neither exactly fitting the image of the typical "nuclear" family. There is nothing "natural" about the family group made up of Dombey, Florence and Walter, little Paul and little Florence. What circulates is not a specific family structure, but a feeling that signifies "family": an image of family in which conflict is absent and in which members are linked by the sharing of feeling, by in fact possessing the same feelings—feelings, not surprisingly, about family. For the novel, the *idea* of family, rather than any particular family structure, signifies; and since "family" exists within each individual, it hardly matters what form it takes externally.

As its critics have noted, *Dombey* offers a critique of personality rather than one of capitalism; once Dombey has lost his pride, business improves.[24] But the novel has never been exactly antibusiness. Rather, it has opposed what it called "unnatural" feelings, the "unnatural" having largely to do with the imposition of will, with "forcing" rather than acceding to "natural" development. At the end of the novel, no forcing is necessary. Sol Gills's investments "turn" of their own accord; Dombey has a source of income which he "has no doubt . . . arises out of some forgotten transaction in the times of the old House" (971). Money is welcome as long as one doesn't investigate its source, and it comes more readily, it seems, when not actively sought. This is how the Midshipman's economy has always operated: *not* selling is rewarded. At the end of the novel, "business" very much resembles Captain Cuttle's fantasy of the Midshipman's new importance to the shipping world: it is "a fiction of a business . . . better than any reality" (972). Similarly, Florence's marriage, which extends the business ("from his daughter, another Dombey and Son will ascend" [974]), is the result of no unnatural transaction but the natural development of her childhood encounter with Walter. *Dombey* traces a movement from rule by force—the repressive, masculine regime of Dombey him-

24. See, for example, Raymond Williams's introduction to the Penguin edition of *Dombey and Son*.

self—to a naturally occurring acceptance of similar values in a regime overseen by Florence, who rules not by force but through nature.[25]

One of the novel's (and one of Dickens's) most famous comments about visibility, the "Oh for a good spirit" passage, ends in a plea for unity. If they could see "what dark shapes issue from amidst their homes. . . . men, delayed no more by stumbling-blocks of their own making, which are but specks of dust upon the path between them and eternity, would then apply themselves, like creatures of one common origin, owing one duty to the Father of one family, and tending to one common end, to make the world a better place!" (738–39). That seeing should lead to "duty," particularly what is described as familial duty, is appropriate to the novel's structuring of knowledge. For *Dombey's* omniscient narration establishes itself by repeatedly insisting upon what Dombey does not know and cannot see.

> When little Florence timidly presented herself, Mr. Dombey stopped in his pacing up and down and looked towards her. Had he looked with greater interest and with a father's eye, he might have read in her keen glance the impulses and fears that made her waver. . . . But he saw nothing of this. (84)

> Oh! Could he have but seen, or seen as others did, the slight spare boy above, watching the waves and clouds at twilight. . . . (236)

---

25. *Dombey and Son* would thus tell the story of a shift from obviously repressive rule (coded male) to a more effective, because less visible, ideological rule (coded female). In an essay on Tennyson, Terry Eagleton writes of the nineteenth century's need to resolve what he calls its oedipus complex: "In striving to achieve its manhood—that is to say, to secure that full political dominance which I will designate as 'masculine'—it needed to settle a certain envying hostility towards its own repressive 'father.' . . . Such iron political repression continues, of course, to be a necessity for the mid-19th-century state; but in so far as this brutally explicit *dominance* fails to secure the conditions of ruling-class *hegemony*, the admiring identification with the strong father must be tempered and complicated by a sustained Oedipal allegiance to the 'mother'—that is to say, to those 'civilising' values of 'sweetness' and 'moral nobility' which are paradigmatically 'feminine.' " See "Tennyson: Politics and Sexuality in 'The Princess' and 'In Memoriam,' " in Francis Barker et al., eds., *The Sociology of Literature: 1848* (Colchester: University of Essex, 1978), p. 97.

For Dombey, Dombey and Son is "the world": "The earth was made for Dombey and Son to trade in, and the sun and moon were made to give them light" (50). Yet the narration insistently points to a larger world that Dombey, and other characters as well, fail to see. Indeed, the novel derives its satiric edge from its technique of presenting characters in relation to what they do not know about themselves, although it sometimes suggests that they can come to possess this knowledge. The "good spirit" passage, for instance, implies that evil need only be made visible in order to be eradicated.

> Oh for a good spirit who would take the house-tops off, with a more potent and benignant hand than the lame demon in the tale, and show a Christian people what dark shapes issue from amidst their homes, to swell the retinue of the Destroying Angel as he moves forth among them! (738)

But more often, the novel suggests that characters may not be able to see, or comprehend, even what is plainly visible.

> Louder and louder yet, it shrieks and cries as it comes tearing on resistless to the goal: and now its way, still like the way of Death, is strewn with ashes thickly. Everything around is blackened. . . . As Mr. Dombey looks out of his carriage window, it is never in his thoughts that the monster who has brought him there has let the light of day in on these things: not made or caused them. (355)

Omniscience can report what everyone sees and can show what "no one" sees, but it cannot make characters see what it reveals. In *Dombey*, responsibility lies not in showing but in seeing, and it is up to characters to learn to see what they need to know. The narrator thus emphasizes his lack of management, an emphasis that is achieved in part through the novel's focus on habit.

According to Morfin, habit keeps individuals from seeing what lies before them.

> I have good reason to believe that a jog-trot life, the same from day to day, would reconcile one to anything. One doesn't see anything, one doesn't hear anything, one doesn't know anything; that's the fact. We go on taking everything for granted,

and so we go on, until whatever we do, good, bad, or indifferent, we do from habit. Habit is all I shall have to report,
when I am called upon to plead to my conscience, on my death-
bed. "Habit," says I; "I was deaf, dumb, blind, and paralytic, to
a million things, from habit." "Very business-like indeed, Mr.
What's-your-name," says Conscience, "but it won't do here!"
(559–60)

Habit encases personality in a predictable, rigid form, in contrast with which the natural is conceived as spontaneous and
unpredictable. It shapes perception, so that characters cannot
see what lies immediately before them, nor can they perceive
the distortions worked upon the natural by unnatural behavior, itself the result of habit.[26] Breaking out of habit—as
Morfin does when he overhears Carker's conversation with
his brother—permits a return to one's "natural" self, at which
time characters will see how unnatural they have become,
finding "a perversion of nature in their own contracted sym-
pathies and estimates" (739). And, having seen the unnatural,
"men, delayed no more by stumbling blocks of their own
making . . . would then apply themselves, like creatures of
one common origin, owing one duty to the Father of one
family, and tending to one common end, to make the world a
better place!" (738–39)

Beyond the father is the Father. Nature, once discovered,
results in unanimity, in the recognition of one's duty to the
Father, which—in the microcosm of the Dombey family—is
the same as duty to the father. The public can no longer
threaten to swallow up the family because the family has
swallowed up the world. The world has been reconceived in
the image of the family.

---

26. The habitual is that which, through repetition, can come to seem
"natural," but is actually, as in Miss Tox's case, a perverse shaping that comes
from too great a concern with public effect.

> From a long habit of listening admiringly to everything that was said in
> her presence, and looking at the speakers as if she were mentally
> engaged in taking off impressions of their images upon her soul, never
> to part with the same but with life, her head had quite settled on one
> side. Her hands had contracted a spasmodic habit of raising them-
> selves of their own accord as in involuntary admiration. (55–56)

It is perhaps not surprising that, having chastised the father with the specter of knowledge greater than his own, the novel ultimately takes the father's part. By attributing Dombey's downfall to his tyranny and obsessiveness, and then asserting "duty to the father" as the highest of values, the novel reflects not just Dickens's own ambivalence about fathers but one characteristic of his age.[27] Punishing an actual father for his tyranny and egotism but also for his fallibility (because he *can* be punished), the novel comes up with an abstraction—an infallible Father—to put in his place, an "other" who, like Florence's fantasies of Dombey, can be fashioned to suit individual desires precisely because of his inaccessibility. Such a father can be suspected of withholding love only because "he did not know how much she loved him. . . . [S]he must try to bring that knowledge to her father's heart one day or other" (423). Such a father's apparent failure, in other words, is always actually one's own. The novel retains the father's repressive rule, but it retains it in the form of ideology—what is internalized and willingly practiced rather than imposed by force. This accounts for the religious feeling of much of the novel's talk about the "remembrance" of little Paul, the eucharistic image of "sharing his heart," and even the internalization of Florence's image. External repression is replaced with a religion of family: the acceptance of, and even desire for, duty to the f(F)ather.

Habit, we are told, only confirms one "in a previous opinion" (51–52). But the narrative's own self-confirmation becomes evident when, in a remarkable moment of unacknowledged self-referentiality, *Dombey*'s narration quotes itself:

"I came, Papa—"
"Against my wishes. Why?" She saw that he knew why: it

27. See Sadoff, *Monsters of Affection,* p. 55, on the idea of the family as devouring all other social institutions. Sadoff also describes "Victorian ambivalence about . . . paternal authority: the desire for its stability, decisiveness, and cultural validity side by side with the hatred of its narrowness, stubbornness, and social domination—oppression—of those without such authority" (6).

was written broadly on his face: and dropped her head upon her hands with one prolonged low cry.

Let him remember it in that room, years to come. It has faded from the air, before he breaks the silence. It may pass as quickly from his brain, as he believes, but it is there. Let him remember it in that room, years to come! (328)

And the ruined man. How does he pass the hours, alone? "Let him remember it in that room, years to come! The rain that falls upon the roof, the wind that mourns outside the door, may have foreknowledge in their melancholy sound. Let him remember it in that room, years to come!"

He did remember it. (934)

To paraphrase Roland Barthes, the very being of omniscience is to keep the question of who is speaking from ever being answered.[28] Quotation, Susan Stewart writes, "points not only inward but outward as well,"[29] establishing a "world within" and one without. Its source unnamed, the quotation naturalizes "foreknowledge"; the narrator's voice might well be "the rain that falls" or "the wind that mourns." It might be, for that matter, the f(F)ather's voice. For the narrator's assertions possess a distinctly fatherly—or Fatherly—tone, stern, parental, and godlike: "Awake, doomed man, while she is near! The time is flitting by; the hour is coming with an angry tread; its foot is in the house. Awake!" (698). The narrator as "father" remains abstract and all-knowing, and what comes to pass, fulfilling his predictions, is presented as affirmation of his authority. The world "without" proves to be as circular and self-enclosed as the world of Dombey and Son. And, like an authoritarian father (and like the police officer who asks if you know why you've been pulled over) the narrator refuses to reveal precisely what it is that one needs to know: what the "it" in "let him remember it" refers to; what it is that "the waves are always saying." What one needs to know, the novel implies, is beyond the capacity of language to represent. Com-

28. Barthes, *S/Z*, p. 140.
29. "What stands outside the quotation mark is seen as spontaneous and original; hence our generic conventions of speaking from the heart, from the body, from nature": Susan Stewart, *On Longing* (Baltimore: Johns Hopkins University Press, 1984), p. 19.

ing to knowledge in *Dombey and Son* means an end to conflict in the discovery of one's duty toward the father and one's familial feeling, the discovery of what the "inner" self has always known and attempted to assert. Dombey's change of feeling, his return to his natural self, is accordingly represented as a dawning recognition: he now knows what he didn't know before; he "remembers it" (935). In other words, what individuals need to know is that which is most natural, and therefore most familial, and which finally comes from within rather than from without. The narrator's knowledge and nature are finally the same. As in the myth of natural development against which the novel opposes such "forcing" establishments as Blimber's Academy, *Dombey and Son* suggests that the natural world is full of voices one may hear only when one has become one's natural self. Finally, it is nature, or natural feeling, that must circulate—even, paradoxically, as it comes from within. And it does so circulate, both inside and outside the novel.

Indeed, both in Dickens's imagination and in fact, the community of feeling created by little Paul's death extends beyond the novel's borders.

> I cannot forego my usual opportunity of saying farewell to my readers in this greeting-place, though I have only to acknowledge the unbounded warmth and earnestness of their sympathy in every stage of the journey we have just concluded.
>
> If any of them have felt a sorrow in one of the principal incidents on which this fiction turns, I hope it may be a sorrow of that sort which endears the sharers in it, one to another. This is not unselfish in me. I may claim to have felt it, at least as much as anybody else; and I would fain be remembered kindly for my part in the experience. (Preface to the 1848 edition)

Dombey and Son reassures its readers, I have argued, on several counts. Most important, it demonstrates the persistence of an "inner life" in a "business" world—a life it constructs according to values of spontaneous emotion and familial feeling. In Dombey's conversion, the novel affirms the persistence of feeling even under the corrupting influence of business—the certainty, for even the most alienated of spectators, of recovering a position within the warmth of family feeling. And, paradoxically claiming communality for the (generally) solitary experience of novel reading, Dickens in his Preface puts the private indulgence of emotion into the service of the family as well. In the world within the novel, a family is restored to natural feeling. And in the world without, a family—invented by Charles Dickens—is created. The novelist becomes the father of a newly forged community founded on feeling he has himself evoked. Thus, although I have suggested that the novel values precisely the non-instrumentality of feeling—what does not circulate—Dickens also provides an explicit use for the feeling the novel summons into existence: the novel and its author become mediators in the formation of an imaginary community. And in the fantasmatic family constructed by *Dombey and Son*, filiation is replaced with familial feeling. Finally, though this family is too vast for its members ever to become acquainted with one another, each member need know of the others only what Edith communicates to Dombey through Florence at the novel's end: that, if Dombey has in fact come to love his daughter, "there is one feeling in common between us now, that there never was before" (968).

But how does the novel circulate what, it claims, must come from within? We might return to the image of invasion for an answer, imagining reading itself as an invasion, in several senses, of privacy, an intrusion into our "private" selves of other beings and other voices. Reading *Dombey*, we—like Dombey—are invaded by Florence's image. But, in the novel's terms, this is the same as being invaded *by* privacy: being possessed by and of an image of the private and natural self which, the novel insists, resides not in the mind but in the breast—where the feelings are ("He hoards her in his heart" [975]).

In a number of ways, both through Dombey's change and through the emotions the novel evokes in its readers, *Dombey and Son* might thus be said to reassure the modern reader, who, according to Sennett, complains, "I never seem to feel enough" (9). For while *Dombey* insists that individuals over-

come the effects of the "jog-trot" life Victorian culture encouraged (or required) them to live, the novel—and not just
Dombey and Son—made itself a habit precisely by offering its
readers a way of doing so. Hochschild's emotional labor thus
has its counterpart in the kind of emotional recreation novels
like *Dombey and Son* provide, recreation that gives readers a
place to experience what is apparently non-instrumental feeling—in other words, feeling that is instrumental precisely
because it appears not to be. Habit was necessary to and
ingrained in individuals by nineteenth-century forms of labor
and recreation, forms to which the serial novel contributed
and on which it depended. In making habit a matter of individual responsibility, however—by emphasizing the individual's need to discover his or her natural self—*Dombey* both
authorizes the kind of anxiety about the self that Sennett
describes and offers itself as remedy.

The personal voice of the Preface differs distinctly from the
managerial voice of the novel's narrator, and the tension between the two might seem to set up a play between business
and the personal. While the novel's omniscient narrator keeps
his distance, the novelist, speaking in his own voice, claims
membership in the community he has created. The distinction
becomes less clear, however, when we consider Dickens's
management of his public persona.

It is a commonplace of Dickens criticism that *Dombey and
Son* inaugurated a new phase in Dickens's career: a return,
after some dabbling in activities such as the editorship of the
Daily News, to novel writing (a movement from business to the
personal), but more than that what Alexander Welsh calls a
"reaffirmation of his vocation" as novelist. Susan Horton
makes much of the idea of "coming home" in her reading of
the novel, while Welsh argues for a shift in biographical emphasis from the blacking warehouse trauma to this period of
what he calls (using Erikson's model of development) a "mor-
atorium" in Dickens's career.[30] Both arguments might be use-

---

30. See Susan Horton, *Interpreting Interpreting* (Baltimore: Johns Hopkins
University Press, 1979); and Alexander Welsh, *From Copyright to Copperfield*

fully glossed by Gabriel Pearson's 1976 essay, "Towards a Reading of *Dombey and Son*," which discusses the deliberateness of Dickens's self-presentation and the ideological nature of the idea of "development."[31] According to Pearson (and as I have argued about the novel's own claims for "nature"), theories of development are no more than myths, interpreting as natural what is ideologically constructed. Where critics typically see a resurgence of the creative artist in this period. Pearson sees a sophisticated manager of his craft, an actor playing "the part of the autonomous creative artist" (57).

In numerous ways—from the management of plot to the management of readers' emotions to the lack of spontaneity in the novel's more "spontaneous" characters—*Dombey*'s critics have found contrivance where the novel celebrates nature. As Pearson points out, Dickens deliberately positioned the deaths of Paul and Mrs. Dombey early in the novel to keep sales high, a response to the disappointing sales of *Martin Chuzzlewit*, the novel immediately preceding *Dombey*. And he describes the "brutal practicality" of the spirit in which Dickens, "apparently with respect to a novel specifically concerned with the evil of money and mercantile pride, decides not to end a monthly number with the spurning and flight of Florence Dombey in order to 'leave a pleasant impression on the reader over Christmas.' "[32] Like Carker, Dickens is in the business of managing feeling; like Florence, however, he manages to make the management of feeling not feel like business, since he only evokes what is already available for evocation "within" each reader: our "sense" of privacy, our "familial feeling."

(Cambridge: Harvard University Press, 1987). The phrase "reaffirmation of his vocation" is from Welsh, p. 10.

31. In Gabriel Josipovici, ed., *The Modern English Novel: The Reader, the Writer and the Work* (London: Open Books, 1976), pp. 54–76.

32. Pearson, "Towards a Reading of *Dombey and Son*," quoting John Butt and Kathleen Tillotson, *Dickens at Work* (London: Methuen, 1963), p. 107. See also Ford, *Dickens and His Readers*, pp. 58–60. On the other hand, Steven Marcus invokes an idea of "natural" genius when he writes that "this is the first of Dickens's novels whose movement seems to obey the heavy, measured pull of some tidal power" (*Dickens: From Pickwick to Dombey*, p. 296).

But, as the personal tone of the 1848 Preface suggests, it may be impossible to separate "business" from the "personal"—in an age of business, in the person of Charles Dickens, or in any age and any person. How does privacy become a sense but through habit? How does the "unnatural" become "natural," and who is to say when it has? What *is* "unnatural" feeling? The very desire to separate inside from outside, within from without, involves us in the same effort I have just deconstructed: the effort to recover a natural self behind the facade of business.

Thus Pearson's essay, while admirably suspicious of the appearance of "natural" feeling, reveals in its evident anger at Dickens's calculations a desire for precisely such feeling: a nostalgia for what, as I hope I have shown, may not exist except as it is constructed through the kinds of oppositions *Dombey* sets up—that may not exist, in other words, except as a result of management.[33] Rather than accuse the novel and its author of hypocrisy, then—the perhaps inevitable hypocrisy wherein a novel that celebrates spontaneity is itself anything but spontaneous—we might simply find contradiction: a novel that denigrates the flow of commerce in which it is itself caught up, and affirms the value of the private self even as it circulates privacy among its readers. Such contradictions are engendered by a culture that demands autonomy and spontaneity in art and artist—that wants to believe in the possibility of non-instrumental feeling—and at the same time offers individuals the opportunity to demonstrate their belief in these qualities in the marketplace. For what has value, the novel insists, does not circulate: "no one, except Florence, knows the measure of the white-haired gentleman's affection for the girl. That story never goes about" (975).

33. Thus Hochschild: "[W]hat we think of as intrinsic to feeling or emotion may have always been shaped to social form and put to civic use" (*The Managed Heart*, p. 18).

(4)

David Copperfield and Bleak House
On Dividing the Responsibility of Knowing

Whether I shall turn out to be the hero of my own life, or whether that station will be held by anybody else, these pages must show.

David Copperfield

As if this narrative were the narrative of *my* life!

Bleak House

Both these remarks—the first opening David Copperfield's recollections, the second occurring early in Esther Summerson's—call into question what we might think we could take for granted: the status of the first-person narrator as the subject of his or her own narrative. The speaker's place is immediately posed as a problem for the narrative; that place, we are invited to suppose, might be occupied by someone else. Nevertheless, readers tend to feel that the possibility being held out to them is merely rhetorical: that what they are about to read is, in fact, the narrator's own history. The gesture of self-effacement therefore tends to be naturalized, incorporated into the narrator's personality. In David's case, for example, it is seen as an indication of modesty; in Esther's, of repression. But what belongs to character here, and what to the exigencies of the narrator's position? David Copperfield and Esther Summerson display the same desire to avoid the constructedness of character that we observed in the *Sketches* and *The Old Curiosity Shop*. And for both, self-effacement functions not chiefly as an aspect of character—modesty or coyness—but as a narrative strategy.

David Copperfield's displacements have led to the critical assessment of him as a figure who is, as D. A. Miller puts it, "not there." Barry Westburg writes that David has a "tendency to associate symbolically with others at critical moments." Robert E. Lougy and David Simpson, among others, call Steerforth and Ham "projections" (although without conveying a clear sense of the tensions involved in discussing characters as "characters" *and* as "projections"). Dickens, Lougy argues, "projects David outside himself and allows us to view David seeing himself, so to speak." "David is but one half of the verb substantive, first person," writes Simpson; "Ham is the figure who is, both physically and thematically, built for the certitude of action from which David's own career remains strangely distant." And Mark Spilka calls *David Copperfield* a "projective novel," one in which "surface life reflects the inner self."[1] Clearly, these critics are talking about the same phenomenon, all registering something incomplete about David Copperfield as a character—namely, that what would make him a character can be found more substantially elsewhere: in other characters. Critics have made similar remarks about Esther Summerson. According to W. J. Harvey, for example, Dickens "chooses to subdue Esther as a character in the interests of her narrative function. We do not, so to speak, look *at* Esther; we look *through* her."[2] In both cases, however, what happens to the idea of "character" if elements that have traditionally been considered oddities of character—coyness, passivity, detachment—are instead viewed as consequences of the narrator's position? For, questioning their own centrality, David and Esther suggest that the villain of one's life—if one is recounting it—is necessarily someone else.

1. Miller, *The Novel and the Police*, p. 215; Barry Westburg, *The Confessional Fictions of Charles Dickens* (De Kalb: Northern Illinois University Press, 1977), p. 83; Robert E. Lougy, "Remembrances of Death Past and Future," *Dickens Studies Annual* 6 (1977): 81; David Simpson, *Fetishism and Imagination: Perception and Representation in the Novels of Dickens, Melville, and Conrad* (Baltimore: Johns Hopkins University Press, 1982), p. 55; and Mark Spilka, "*David Copperfield* as Psychological Fiction," in Dyson, ed., *Dickens: Modern Judgements*, p. 186.
2. W. J. Harvey, *Character in the Novel* (Ithaca: Cornell University Press, 1965), p. 94.

Omniscience is typically associated with inclusiveness. As I have argued, omniscience expresses a fantasy of transcending individual consciousness. Yet both David Copperfield and Esther Summerson represent themselves as inadequate to the worlds they describe. Though David occasionally claims superiority in reading characters' minds, neither he nor Esther Summerson participates in Dickens's fantasy of omniscience by claiming absolute knowledge about their subjects. Rather, they fulfill the observer's role by effacing themselves, both explicitly—as this chapter's epigraphs suggest—and implicitly, since both remain essentially invisible to readers. Self-effacement widens both their own field of vision and the reader's, their immateriality permitting a collapse of the boundary that might separate them from the reader. And their effacement is an effect of the displacement of action and of character. The "fantasy of omniscience" refers, in this chapter, not to a pretense to absolute knowledge, but rather to omniscience's typical displacements, projections, and disavowals of agency: the suggestion that no one sees, describes, or constructs.

These narratives are not, of course, omniscient in any ordinary sense of the term. But their narrators locate in other characters qualities that demonstrably belong to the narrators themselves. As such, they invite comparison with Dickens's technically omniscient narratives, which similarly displace the personal. Gesturing away from themselves, these narrators make other characters the chief actors in their narratives; their immateriality enables the evasion of character, with all its Dickensian implications. Esther and David construct themselves, and we see them, through a series of reflections and displacements, as other characters act out a drama which frees these narrators from the consequences of action and of knowledge.

And yet these narratives differ from omniscient ones in several important ways. Unlike omniscience, first-person narration invites the possibility of reversal. Even as the narrator occupies the transcendent position, the existence of the "I" raises the possibility that the "I" may become "you"—that the subject is in danger of becoming an object for someone else, or is, perhaps, already and inescapably an object for someone else.[3] First-person narrative thus makes explicit what omniscient narration obscures: that the subject of narrative is also a potential object of it. And yet, as subjects and objects of their own narratives, first-person narrators occupy a position of self-transcendence. In fact, the tension these narrators display between "limitation," typically considered the defining attribute of the first-person narrator, and the transcendence the narrator's position enables, points toward the way omniscience may usefully be regarded not as a fixed technique— the absence of an "I"—but as a fantasy narrative makes it possible to indulge. For both "first-person" and "omniscient" narrators, narrating involves the desire to take up a position outside the self.

These narratives are also explicitly gendered, each shaped by the requirements of the period's gender systems. Gender difference is registered, for instance, in David Copperfield's description of himself as invisible eye, a consciousness coincident with the act of seeing ("if I lost sight of anything for a moment, I was gone" [65]), while Esther Summerson—equally invisible to readers—nevertheless describes herself as existing *because she is seen.* The difference between David's easy analogy between what exists and what he sees, and Esther's conceptualization of herself as object of the gaze, goes some distance toward explaining the implicitly masculine perspective of Dickens's omniscient narratives. These first-person narratives thus suggest what omniscience has already shown: that the subject of narrative can imaginatively avoid becoming a character in someone else's narrative simply by making others into characters in his or her own story. But in so doing, they also reveal their subjects to be constructed by agencies not under their control, to be "characters in a cultural script" written by others as they write themselves.[4]

3. In discussing the reversibility of "I" and "you," Emile Benveniste provides a model for the tensions within first-person narration. Though he claims that "I" and "you" are reversible, he also argues that " 'I' is always transcendent with respect to 'you.' " Reversibility does not mean equality, but rather inequality: the one who says "I" defines the other as "not-I." See "Relationships of Person in the Verb," (in *Problems in General Linguistics*), pp. 198–201.
4. The phrase comes from Nina Auerbach, "Alluring Vacancies in the Victorian Character," *Kenyon Review* 8 (1986): 46.

DAVID COPPERFIELD

In *David Copperfield*, as in the *Sketches*, the unformedness of a narrator who "never thought of anything about myself, distinctly" (272), contrasts starkly with the clearly drawn characters he describes, characters defined in terms of physical and psychological marks and habits. To be a character in *David Copperfield* is to be formed, and to be formed, as Clara Copperfield's fate alone would demonstrate, is to be subjected to another's vision, another's narrative.

For David Copperfield, character is always a problematic proposition. As a child, he has before him two models: the weakness of his mother and the firmness that makes such weakness its target. And character in this novel takes shape in degrees of, and in responses to, Murdstonian firmness.

> Mr. Murdstone was firm; nobody in his world was to be as firm as Mr. Murdstone; nobody else in his world was to be firm at all, for everybody was to be bent to his firmness. Miss Murdstone was an exception. She might be firm, but only by relationship, and in an inferior and tributary degree. My mother was another exception. She might be firm, and must be; but only in bearing their firmness, and firmly believing there was no other firmness upon earth. (99)

David's choice appears to be one of harming others or being harmed by them, of victimizing or being victimized. And victimization—being the object of firmness—is identified with being closely watched. The Murdstones' surveillance turns David's home into a prison and David himself into a "guarded captive" (102). Peggoty declares that the sister sleeps "with one eye open" (98), and Murdstonian watching keeps David from expressing affection for his mother ("I knew quite well that he was looking at us both" [93]).[5]

David's response to being watched is to become a watcher himself. Defining himself as such from the very first moments

---

5. Pearl Chesler Solomon writes of David's "determination not to be victimized" in *Dickens and Melville in Their Time* (New York: Columbia University Press, 1975), p. 148.

of the novel, he is an especially keen observer in relation to
Murdstone.

> Mr. Murdstone and I were soon off, and trotting along on the
> green turf by the side of the road. . . . I could not make up my
> mind to sit in front of him without turning my head sometimes,
> and looking up in his face. He had that kind of shallow black
> eye . . . which, when it is abstracted, seems from some pecu-
> liarity of light to be disfigured, for a moment at a time, by a cast.
> (71)

Watching the watcher, David responds to a world in which
power manifests itself as vision, in which it seems that a
character can avoid being subjected to the structuring gazes of
others only by remaining aware of their watching and by
watching them in return. The narrative sets up an epistemological battle in which character and narrator vie for this transcendent position, and yet the fact that such a battle takes
place reveals the narrator's tenuous hold, suggesting as it does
the potential reversibility of subject-object positions. The narrator affirms his position by representing himself representing
others, in an effort to establish himself as unconstrained by
them.

David avoids firmness of character in two ways: by presenting himself as "meandering" narrator and by "picturing" himself. In the first case, we are presented with a gaze that refuses
to structure what it encounters: the eye simply wanders, de-
tailing what it sees. At the very beginning of his narrative,
David recounts the story of the caul with which he was born,
supposed to preserve its owner from death by drowning. The
old woman who buys it—he reflects uneasily on the "dis-
posal" of "a part of myself" (50)—considers herself safe because she has avoided meandering about the world, and repeats the injunction, "Let us have no meandering." (The sale
of the caul is, however, itself a kind of meandering: a dispersal
or fragmentation of self, as well as a seeing of part of the self
from the outside.) But the admonition merely points to what it
prohibits. In fact, David frequently meanders, particularly
when enjoined not to: in church ("I look at my mother. . . . I

look at a boy. . . . I look at the sunlight" [64]) or while reciting his lessons ("I think of the number of yards of net in Miss Murdstone's cap, or of the price of Mr. Murdstone's dressing-gown" [104]). He meanders, that is, directly in response to the threat of being confined.

David's meandering narrative may be seen as a refusal to be the self the Murdstones want him to be. The subject who meanders remains undefined. Always in the process of over-flowing his boundaries, he is neither constrained nor con-tained, his vision identified simply with what exists. But while meandering narrative refuses to fix boundaries, it also, David claims, signifies his inability to delimit others, a phenomenon which he describes in terms of entrapment: "I could observe, in little pieces, as it were; but as to making a net of a number of those pieces, and catching anybody in it, that was, as yet, beyond me" (70). But even meandering observation forms a net in which others are caught. Unfocused as David's percep-tions may appear to be, they fashion a net out of representa-tion itself. And only by representing others can the narrator avoid being caught in that net himself.

After Murdstone beats him, David looks "at his face in the glass, so swollen, red, and ugly that it almost frightened me" (108). When he speaks of being punished by Creakle, we learn that he is "chubby" (141). The fact that David becomes visible as a character only when marked by a beating underscores the equation this novel establishes between markedness and con-straint. Disfiguration—here and in *Bleak House*—signals both the character's bounded subjectivity and the narrator's posi-tion outside it, appearing in Dickens's work as the antithesis of the narrator's invisibility: as a figure for being written into the text.[6] The marked character, in other words, is a metaphor for

6. Helena Michie argues that "the female self, like Dickens' female charac-ters, comes into being through illness, scarring, and deformity." But the evidence of *David Copperfield* suggests that in the novel character is itself a scar, a "marking" of identity by an effaced narrator. As D. A. Miller writes: "The contrast [is] . . . inscribed within the nineteenth-century novel as one be-tween the character and the narrator, our readerly surrogate and point of view, who is in general so shadowy and indeterminate a figure that it scarcely

character *as* mark. When forced to wear the placard "He Bites," David experiences himself as, in essence, a written character—"Whether it was possible for people to see me or not, I always fancied that someone was reading it"—and begins "to have a dread of myself, as a kind of wild boy who did bite" (131). Being read by others is associated both with the anxiety of being watched and with punishment. It is no wonder that, when David reads, he makes the Murdstones into characters in his books, "putting Mr. and Miss Murdstone into all the bad ones" (106). He again hints at this strategy of revenge via narrative in the "Brooks of Sheffield" incident, when Murdstone and his cohorts expose David's naïveté by making him into a character in their narrative: the "sharp" Brooks of Sheffield. Revealing his sharpness by telling the story, David turns them all into characters in *his* book.

But David also uses the divided self that his autobiographical narrative produces—his status as character in his own story—to create a narrative self far removed from objectification. Seeing himself in the mirror after Murdstone's beating, he is "almost frightened" of his own face; wearing the placard, he has "a dread of myself." As narrator, he can "picture" himself, differentiating himself from a past self with whom he no longer coincides. When, in *Master Humphrey's Clock*, Humphrey remembers his mother in the context of her death and describes a group of children who resemble "angels" pictured in a book his mother holds, he realizes, as he refers back and forth between the children and the book, that his own deformed self is not represented in it. The scene dramatizes a desire for presence as well as for absence: the fact that it is

---

seems right to call him a person at all. But Dickens's fiction is particularly relevant to the problematics of modern subjectivity, because his novels pose such a sharp contrast in the extreme difference and distance between the character, who is so thoroughly extroverted that his inner life seems exiguous, and the narrator, who is so completely defaced that, even when he bears a name like David Copperfield, Phiz hardly knows what 'phiz' to give him." See Michie, " 'Who Is This in Pain': Scarring, Disfigurement, and Female Identity in *Bleak House* and *Our Mutual Friend*," *Novel* 22 (1989): 199; and Miller, *The Novel and the Police*, p. 209.

Humphrey's birthday places him at the emotional center of events, while the discovery of the missing representation marks both a loss and an empowerment. Absent, he becomes the scene's omniscient narrator, central to it and yet invisible in it. In *David Copperfield*, the mother's death is again linked with the narrator's birth—the birth, that is, of a self existing apart from the mother, an image not in her eyes but in the eyes of others. David is at school when he learns of his mother's death, and when he sees the other boys watching him, his grief is transformed into a sense of self-importance:

> If ever child were stricken with sincere grief, I was. But I remember that this importance was a kind of satisfaction to me, when I walked in the playground that afternoon while the boys were in school. When I saw them glancing at me out of the windows, as they went up to their classes, I felt distinguished, and looked more melancholy, and walked slower. (177)

His mother's death provides for David a differentiated self, an awareness of what he looks like to others, which also establishes a difference within the self. While the scene in *Master Humphrey* involves the disappearance of the self as object, the *David Copperfield* passage describes the development of a sense of theatricality which also permits the avoidance of objectification.[7] Conscious of his ability to manipulate appearance, David feels not so much his own grief as the desire to present an appearance of grief to others. To have others see him truly grieving would involve the danger of objectification, but to present an appearance of grief is to avert that danger. Others see only what he wants them to see, what he is aware that they are seeing. He remains at the center of the scene, but only in a sense: at the center is David the character. The David who truly feels grief has, at least for the moment, disappeared. Thus as David Copperfield's narrative doubles him, establishing him as both character and narrator, the character is caught

7. This, it seems to me, is the mistake Robert Garis (*The Dickens Theatre*) makes in equating egotism with love of performance. Garis fails to see that performance or theatricality can be a means of concealing what he calls the "inner self" rather than evidence of its absence.

in the net of representation while the narrator has by definition transcended representation. And the invisibility of the
one is enabled by the visibility of the other.

David thus avoids being constituted as a fixed subject in
part by representing another David within the text: a self set
firmly in the past, which is, at the very moment of its representation, displaced. For, as narrator, David is always detached from the self he pictures, by virtue of picturing it.

> I picture my small self in the dimly lighted rooms, sitting with
> my head upon my hand. . . . I picture myself with my books
> shut up, still listening to the doleful performance of Mr. Mell.
> (132)

It is by means of such picturing—such seeing the self from
without—that, according to Lacan, the subjective self comes
into being. Yet implicit in this movement, and in vision itself
(as Christian Metz has written of the cinema), is distance, for
the self that can picture is by definition outside, and thus no
longer coincident with, the self it pictures.[8]

> I look down on the line of boys below me, with a condescend-
> ing interest in such of them as bring to my mind the boy I was
> myself, when I first came there. That little fellow seems to be no
> part of me; I remember him as something left behind upon the
> road of life—as something I have passed, rather than have
> actually been—and almost think of him as someone else. (325)

As in the case of the caul, this scene presents the past self as
a lost "part of me," a fragment no longer belonging to the
speaker. At the same time, David's picturing is here characterized by the absence of any picture: the passage provides no
visual image. Even as David the narrator depicts David the
character, he defends that character against representation.

Picturing his younger self and other characters allows
David to subordinate them as objects, to exercise narrative
control over them while remaining open and undefined in
relation to them. And in general David presents his past life as
a series of tableaux. After his mother's death, "the idea of her

8. Metz, *The Imaginary Signifier*, ch. 3.

as she had been of late vanished from me. I remembered her, from that instant, only as the young mother of my earliest impressions, who had been used to wind her bright curls round and round her finger, and to dance with me at twilight in the parlour" (186). And the chapter in which Clara Copperfield's death occurs is surrounded by assurances that others will remain "the same" to him. If he has any fears that Peggotty's marriage will result in his abandonment, as his mother's did, he quickly establishes that "if Peggotty had been married every day for the last ten years, she could hardly have been more at her ease about it; it made no sort of difference in her; she was just the same as ever" (201). The effect of Steerforth's death is similarly to freeze his image as it was in David's youth: "I saw him lying with his head upon his arm, as I had often seen him lie at school" (866). Robin Gilmour calls David's evocation of such scenes an "imaginative identification with states of feeling which . . . works against the tone of mellow acceptance that the adult, domesticated David assumes,"[9] but this assessment fails to account for the distance these scenes suggest, a distance David explicitly compares to theater: "I was so filled with the play, and with the past—for it was, in a manner, like a shining transparency, through which I saw my earlier life moving along" (345).

In the series of "Retrospect" chapters, David considers the difference between his past and present life, taking note of those who have assisted in his development. At the end of the novel, as he looks for familiar faces "in the fleeting crowd" (946), characters again come forth as if to reassure him of their sameness: Peggotty still holds the Crocodile Book; Rosa Dartle and Mrs. Steerforth endlessly repeat the discovery of Steerforth's death. And while asserting the sameness of other characters he notes the changes in his own nature, the narrative thus opposing David's changing self to the habitual nature of the characters he describes. While he wonders "what nature and accident had made me" so as to "be that, and nothing

---

9. Robin Gilmour, "Memory in *David Copperfield*," *Dickensian* 71 (1975): 38. Subsequent references in text.

else" (758), other characters reassure him that they remain as they always were. Likewise, while others characters suffer the consequences of their actions, the narrator gets a second chance; what he imagines as "those things that never happen" (891) do, for him, take place. David's position as spectator of his earlier life contradicts arguments such as Gilmour's, which see the novel's narrative movement as "a return from a secure present . . . to a less secure but more vital and complex past" (31). For David returns to his past in order to fix it and to experience it as fixed, thereby establishing his present distance from it.[10]

This same desire to fix character in others—and to fix others as characters—appears in David's account of the origin of his writing career. He locates the beginnings of his ambition in a series of scenes in which he watches others "file past in review" while he makes up stories about them. In Micawber's prison cell, as David retrospectively views the scene, Micawber's fellow inmates "come filing before me in review again," and he associates them with the development of his "imaginative world" (225). In these scenes characters perform their identities, as the future writer, displaying no identity but that of recorder, looks on.

The clearest example of the contrast between David's ability to change and the fixedness of the characters he describes is found in his marriage to Agnes, who waits for him, her feelings unaltered, as he undergoes his numerous alterations. It thus makes sense that when, toward the end of the novel, he imagines that he has made an irrevocable mistake and finds himself left with "two irreconcilable conclusions" (765), he discovers that the only rival he has for Agnes is himself. The apparently irreconcilable can, if one is narrating one's own life, be reconciled.

The subject of autobiography who attempts to construct his

10. Barry Westburg writes that the characters in David's narrative "all coexist in a kind of eternal suspension, ready to go into their acts whenever the hero needs them." David has, as Westburg aptly puts it, "his past on tap." See *The Confessional Fictions*, p. 51.

or her narrative as a suspenseful one—refusing to tell the end of the story—is in the peculiar position of knowing and not knowing at once, or, more precisely, of knowing but attempting to appear not to know. But David is not simply in the business of producing suspense. His depiction of himself as unknowing and innocent also keeps him free of the consequences of knowledge and action. Like an omniscient narrator, David evades responsibility for what he recounts; as narrator, he purports simply to recount what he observes.[11] But that posture is often at odds with the presence of a more controlling narrator, one who explicitly determines what readers and other characters will know.

David is occasionally quite explicit about his control of knowledge, his ability to conceal his thoughts from characters and readers. Of Mr. Peggoty, for example, he writes, "I believe that his honest heart was transparent to me," moments before reflecting, "I made no other comment on this information than that I supposed he would see her soon. Such speculations as it engendered within me I kept to myself, and those were faint enough" (781–83). He records Emily's "confidence" about Martha, as well as his deliberation not to reveal it to Steerforth, thus: "I made a resolution, therefore, to keep it in my own breast; and there it gave her image a new grace" (401). Here David deliberately suppresses knowledge, and tells us that he does so. But at other moments, recording events or details that seem meaningful because he records them, he does not make their significance explicit. This narrative strategy blurs the difference between suppression and repression. David's assertion in some instances that he withholds information implies that, where that assertion is absent, he is telling us everything he knows. Thus by asserting his narratorial control David makes room for what appears to be lack of control, for the element of unknowingness that keeps him distanced from the narrative's conflicts. It is "sharp" of him, for example, to re-

11. For a discussion of David as "young" in relation to the issue of class in the novel, see John Jordan, "The Social Sub-Text of *David Copperfield*," *Dickens Studies Annual* 14 (1985): 61–92.

count the "Brooks of Sheffield" incident, and yet, identifying with his childhood self as he recounts it, he appears unaware of his sharpness. We thus see him as Murdstone's victim even as, telling the story, he succeeds in making Murdstone and his cronies objects of his apparently innocent representation.

It is in fact David's identification with his childhood self that often makes him appear an innocent observer, revealing to readers more than he himself is able to understand.

> Gradually, I became used to seeing the gentleman with the black whiskers. I liked him no better than at first, and had the same uneasy jealousy of him; but if I had any reason for it beyond a child's instinctive dislike . . . it certainly was not *the* reason that I might have found if I had been older. (70)

But the David telling the story *is* older. Identification with the younger self is more than an attempt to create an effect of verisimilitude, in which the form of the narrative imitates that of the life. Rather, such identification defines the narrator as both unwilling and unable to articulate the implications of what he sees.

Thus seeing does not imply an elucidation of what, having been seen, is known. David Copperfield's position as one who controls the reader's knowledge is at odds with his desire to remain untainted by the possession of certain kinds of knowledge. What a child can do without explanation becomes a problem for the adult narrator. Much of what David learns as an adult, he therefore learns, we are told, "by accident." Although as a child, for instance, he actively watches Murdstone and Creakle, he later disavows even the deliberate act of looking: "I looked at nothing, that I know of, but I saw everything" (463). He represents himself as passively learning of Little Em'ly "what she had been unable to repress when her heart lay open to me by an accident" (401). And his accidental position behind the door in the scene between Rosa Dartle and Emily permits him to witness what is intended for no one else's eyes or ears. In fact, David's narrative, like Boz's, is littered with excuses for his presence. "I found myself among them" (398); "My aunt and I came to be left together near the door" (724). We can see in these phrases the rationale behind one of Dickens's early titles for the novel: "The Copperfield Survey of the World as it Rolled." As surveyor of the world, David need not "own" what he sees; what he sees is simply "the world" ("I remark this, because I remark everything that happens" [184]). Yet, as the change in title tells us, this is also his personal history. The tension between the subjective observer and a distant and dispassionate perspective which would represent "the world" is, of course, characteristic of Dickens's omniscience. Presenting David as "accidental" narrator of much of the novel, Dickens leaves unclear what belongs to David's story—what is part of him—and what isn't. The title change reflects the peculiar tension between the distance David wants to have on the material he observes and the fact that this material is, at the same time, his life.

As he describes events between Annie Strong and the Doctor (which he witnesses, again, by accident), David can say only that he saw in Annie's face "that horror of I don't know what" (304). And the older Copperfield participates in the disavowal: "Distinctly as I recollect her look, I cannot say of what it was expressive, I cannot even say of what it is expressive to me now" (304). Unwilling or unable to say, the narrator remains innocent of suspecting Annie and of the knowledge such suspicion would entail. This disavowal of knowledge about potential triangularities is most useful, of course, in relation to Steerforth and Em'ly. The "unconscious part" David played in Steerforth's "pollution of an honest home" (516) can remain (if uneasily) unconscious, and David in no danger of being accused of responsibility. Having introduced Steerforth and Em'ly to one another and having mediated their relationship, he cannot be said to accept, or, as the narrative presents it, to bear any responsibility for subsequent events.

David's evasion of his activity as observer is thus an evasion of the ownership of knowledge. But what he knows, but cannot or will not articulate, other characters make explicit. In the latter half of the novel, Uriah plays "I" to David's "you," raising for David the possibility of reversibility, and threatening, as Murdstone did earlier, to make David a character in a narrative not his own—or rather, to make David acknowledge that everything in the narrative *is* his own. When Uriah reveals his suspicions about Annie to the Doctor and attempts to identify David as secretly sharing them, David is caught between acknowledgment and disavowal. "Since we have got so far," says Uriah, "I ought to take the liberty of mentioning that Copperfield has noticed it too" (682). "You know," he says, addressing David, "you knew what I meant."

> I saw the mild eye of the good old Doctor turned upon me for a moment, and I felt that the confession of my old misgivings and remembrances was too plainly written in my face to be overlooked. It was of no use raging. I could not undo that. Say what I would, I could not unsay it. (683)

Marked by "that horror of I don't know what," David becomes something like a character in Uriah's script, a figure in a text to be read by others. His discomfort takes precedence over the Doctor's distress, the scene instead emphasizing the unpleasantness and yet the inevitability of the fact that David can't help seeing, in Uriah's face, "what I already knew." The contest between the two is one of ambition and sexuality, but it is staged at this point as a contest about knowledge: "He knew me better than I knew myself" (687). And yet even as he acknowledges that he and Uriah share knowledge, David won't define what that knowledge is, or how he comes to know it. He makes himself the passive victim not only of Uriah, but of knowledge itself. Confessing that "the strange feeling (to which, perhaps, no one is quite a stranger) that all this had occurred before, at some indefinite time, and that I knew what he was going to say next, took possession of me" (441), he evades the moment's implications by representing knowledge as seizing him, rather than the other way round.

As a number of critics have noted, Uriah embodies qualities that David refuses to acknowledge in himself—in particular, social ambition. This scene comes close to affirming the likeness between the two, but it defers recognition. Instead we see Uriah as a version of the "swollen, red, and ugly" scar inflicted on David by Murdstone, the disfigured self the narrator will not recognize as his own. David appears as Uriah's victim, compelled to reveal thoughts better left unexpressed, and Uriah is cast as the villain for forcing them to the surface. His own representational strategy unremarked, the narrator appears to be the innocent object of another's machinations.

David's encounter with Uriah interestingly resembles that moment in *Bleak House* in which Esther Summerson encounters her mother face-to-face for the first time. Like David Copperfield, Esther locates in other characters what she does not want to acknowledge in herself. But where David must deny his ambition, ostensibly succeeding because he is earnest rather than aggressive, Esther, in order to occupy her proper social place, must deny what the novel represents as illicit sexuality and attaches to the figure of her mother.

BLEAK HOUSE

Whereas *David Copperfield* attempts to collapse the distance and difference between the individual subject and the world, *Bleak House* insists on their separation. In this novel, third-person, omniscient, "impersonal" narration has one place, and limited, individualized, "personal" narration another. But what does it mean for omniscience to have a place? The double narrative, constituting as it does a boundary omniscience cannot cross, raises a problem for the very notion of omniscience. Though the contrast with Esther's narrative contributes to the other narrative's omniscient effect, the presence of her narrative also suggests its limitations. Omniscience in *Bleak House* is paradoxically proscribed, limited to one half of the novel.[12] The idea of omniscience as all-knowing is thus undermined by

---

12. I do not mean that the omniscient narrative cannot deal with material also appearing in Esther's narrative; of course, it does. But the elaboration of Esther's point of view is given to us as something the omniscient narrative cannot contain within itself, and which therefore needs to be located elsewhere.

I use the term "omniscient" for this narrative not because I believe that it "is" omniscient, but because I believe that Dickens meant it to be taken as such. It is no more or less "omniscient" than any of the other narratives discussed here.

Esther's narrative, which, as supplement, to use Derrida's term, reveals a lack in what is supposed to be complete.[13] And the existence of Esther's narrative immediately suggests the possibility of other narratives: Richard's, Ada's, Jarndyce's, Guppy's. Thus although omniscience need not signify only distance—indeed, the term implies the ability to move inside and outside character—in *Bleak House*, it seems, omniscience cannot "do" the personal.

The kind of supplementary relationship the split narration of *Bleak House* suggests, in which one part supplies knowledge the other doesn't possess, or in which two halves appear to make up a whole, appears in other forms throughout the novel. The Bagnets, the Badgers, the Smallweeds, the Jelly-bys—even Boythorn and his bird, Bucket and his finger—are similarly divided entities, in which one member of the couple either speaks for the other (the Bagnets), or represents a kind of complement to the other (as Mr. Jellyby's silence does to Mrs. Jellyby's busyness), or metonymically expresses what is hidden within the other (the way Bucket's finger represents his seemingly magical powers, or Boythorn's bird reveals his gentleness). In form, as split subjects whose parts do not acknowledge or fail to know one another, these characters reproduce the novel's divided structure.[14]

13. See Jacques Derrida, *Of Grammatology*, trans. Gayatri Spivak (Baltimore: Johns Hopkins University Press, 1976), pp. 141–57.

14. There is little agreement about the nature of and relationship between *Bleak House*'s two narratives. Catherine Belsey states bluntly, "Neither is omniscient," without arguing the point. J. Hillis Miller writes that "both narrators hide as much as they reveal" (though "hiding" does not obviate omniscience). For Ellen Serlen the impersonal narration is an objective, impersonal eye representing what we are meant to understand as the "real" world; for John Lucas, who seems to consider the narrator a person, "the narrator's poised and comprehensive knowledge give him an authority we do not feel ourselves in a position to challenge." Taylor Stoehr, however, claims that the third-person narrator only possesses knowledge of the present. And while Serlen finds Esther's narrative obviously unreliable, for W. J. Harvey, Esther "offers us stability, a point of rest in a flickering and bewildering world, the promise of some guidance through the labyrinth." G. Armour Craig finds that the two narratives are separated by "a gulf . . . greater than can be bridged by any connection," though many critics seem able to discuss the difference between the same events as reported in each narrative. Together, writes Peter

Given one narrative that, we are explicitly told, someone has written, we are also offered one that it seems no one has—at least no human agent who will acknowledge it. This general premise is so compelling that readers tend not to care about those ways in which the fiction sustaining each narrative cannot be upheld: about the fact that the third-person narrator speaks, for a moment, in the first person (620), or about the numerous times when Esther's "little body" does "fall into the background," as she says (74)—times when she records conversations in such detail that, if the narrative's premise is to make sense, we must imagine either that she writes constantly or possesses an uncanny capacity for memorization. For much of her narrative, that is, Esther might as well be omniscient.

At times, the tension between Esther's role as character and her role as narrator places her in an awkward position, as, for instance, when she sits with Richard and Ada:

> I had never seen any young people falling in love before, but I found them out quite soon. I could not say so, of course, or show that I knew anything about it. On the contrary, I was so demure, and used to seem so unconscious, that sometimes I considered within myself while I was sitting at work, whether I was not growing quite deceitful. (163)

What are we to make of the relationship between character and narrator in this passage, in which the former's meekness or "unconsciousness" is subverted by the latter's active mind and eye? Telling what she knows, making it clear that she knows, Esther speaks at the same time of her need to remain "in character." But her qualms about deceitfulness, like Flor-

Garrett, the two narratives give us a sense of "alternate versions of meaning . . . the sense that every event or relationship is subject to opposed interpretations." Catherine Belsey, *Critical Practice* (London: Methuen, 1980), p. 80; J. Hillis Miller, introduction to Penguin edition of *Bleak House*, p. 13; John Lucas, *The Melancholy Man* (London: Methuen, 1970), p. 211; Ellen Serlen, "The Two Worlds of *Bleak House*," *ELH* 43 (1976): pp. 551–66; Taylor Stoehr, *Dickens: The Dreamer's Stance*, p. 147; W. J. Harvey, "Chance and Design in *Bleak House*," in Gross and Pearson, eds., *Dickens and the Twentieth Century*, p. 152; G. Armour Craig, "The Unpoetic Compromise," in Jacob Korg, ed., *Twentieth-Century Interpretations of Bleak House* (Englewood Cliffs, N.J.: Prentice-Hall, 1968), p. 60; and Peter Garrett, *The Victorian Multiplot Novel*, p. 59.

ence Dombey's when she catches a glimpse of Carker leaving Dombey's house, register the tension produced in these figures by their double role as observers—narrators or narratorial surrogates—and as characters. And that tension is registered throughout *Bleak House* as a tension within character alone: Esther is presented as a split subject, divided from herself. But narratological structures may appear as what we call psychological ones; the narratological and the psychological may be mutually determining. The detachment from and denial of knowledge expressed here at the level of individual character reproduces the structure of detachment and denial exemplified in the novel's double narration. In other words, Esther's detached relationship to her own knowledge, like that of those other fragmented characters described above, may be seen as a version of the novel's more general displacement of knowledge and responsibility—a displacement expressed most powerfully by the way in which the two narratives, in the words of the character Vholes, "divide the responsibility of knowing" (672).

Knowledge—both its discovery and its ownership—is clearly a problem in *Bleak House*. The word "know" echoes throughout. "I know so much about so many characters," says Bucket (782). "Not to know that there is something wrong at the Dedlocks' is to augur yourself unknown" (842), the narrator claims. Says Bucket to Esther, "I know, I know, and would I put you wrong, do you think? Inspector Bucket. Now you know me, don't you?" (841). And, of course, "Jarndyce and Jarndyce drones on. . . . [N]o man alive knows what it means" (52). The world of Chancery and the world of fashion, we learn early in the novel, are so separate that neither knows the other; the world of fashion is "wrapped up in too much jeweller's cotton and fine wool, and cannot hear the rushing of the larger worlds" (55). But the narrator can "pass from one to the other, as the crow flies" (55). As in *Dombey*, the third-person narrator establishes his omniscience by moving between worlds that are kept distinct precisely to allow for such movement.

Each narrative, as I have suggested, provides a framework

for and counterpart to the other. In contrast to Esther's narrative, the distant, disembodied third-person narrator easily assumes the position of what Lacan calls *le sujet supposé savoir*. Esther, on the other hand, has all the limitation a critic interested in first-person narration could hope to find; limitation is in fact her chief subject. She is indeed the subject presumed—primarily by herself—not to know.

But, as *David Copperfield* shows, the subject who presents him or herself as not knowing is not the same as the subject who doesn't know. *Bleak House* presents us with one place where knowledge appears to be and another where it does not. But the latter is, rather, a place where knowledge is asserted to be absent. Insisting upon her status as one who does not know, who does not even occupy the subject's position in her narrative, Esther works to efface her own knowledge. And her self-effacing narration serves both a narrative and a characterological purpose, enabling her to structure her narrative and her character without appearing deliberately to do so.

Though Esther is frequently more knowing than it seems her character "should" be, her status as character is confirmed, for readers, by her insistence on her lack of knowledge. If, that is, Esther knows too much, her pathology insists that we forget or ignore her knowledge. As character, denying that she knows, Esther invites readers to feel that they know her better than she knows herself. For her discourse overflows with what is presented as unconscious material, assuming we understand the unconscious to be that which exceeds the subject's own knowledge or control. Our understanding of Esther's knowledge thus necessarily connects with the larger issues of knowledge and responsibility the novel raises.[15] And to explore that relationship more fully requires us to focus both on the way Esther's character is constructed by and founded in language, and on her relationship to her mother,

---

15. On Esther's strategic use of repression, see John Kucich, *Repression in Victorian Fiction* (Berkeley and Los Angeles: University of California Press, 1987), pp. 252–70.

who is essential to Esther's construction of herself as a subject who claims not to know.

In the essay "Negation," Freud describes a characteristic structure whereby unconscious material emerges into discourse. The patient says, " 'You ask who this person in the dream can have been. It was *not* my mother.' We emend this: so it *was* his mother."[16] Denial, according to Freud, permits a dissociation of intellect from affect that allows unconscious material to be spoken. "Negation is a way of taking account of what is repressed; indeed, it is already a lifting of the repression, though not, of course, an acceptance of what is repressed. . . . The outcome of this is a kind of intellectual acceptance of the repressed, while at the same time what is essential to the repression persists" (235–36). Freud claims that such statements of negation—what Lacan, combining the terms "denial" and "negation," calls "denegations"—derive from judgments about what the ego wishes to take into itself and what it wishes to reject. And judgment, the decision about what is "good" or "bad," is for Freud an extension of the pleasure principle. If we accept Freud's argument, then, intellectual judgment can be said to be the distant relation of pleasure or unpleasure. "Good" and "bad" signify what "I should like to take . . . into myself" and what I wish "to keep . . . out" (237).

Denegation is a particularly prevalent form of rhetoric in *Bleak House*, presented to us ironically in the speech of such characters as Vholes and Skimpole. It is Vholes's distinctive habit, for instance, to assert his disinterest in Richard's case, on which he is employed. He exemplifies the novel's critique of "duty," the attempt to dissociate interest from personal connections and feeling. Yet Vholes has "interests" which he readily admits to even while he denies them: "I have no interest in it," he says of the case, "except as a member of society and a father—*and* a son" (672). In other words, he has nothing

16. Sigmund Freud, "Negation," in *The Standard Edition of the Complete Psychological Works of Sigmund Freud*, ed. James Strachey, 24 vols. (London: Hogarth Press, 1966), vol. 19, p. 235. Subsequent references included in text.

but interest in it— interest which, he means to say, is his own rather than Richard's. Attempting to distinguish between his interest and Richard's, however, Vholes succeeds rather in suggesting the extent to which the two are intertwined. The denial of interest does not, in *Bleak House*, mean disinterest, but usually its opposite. In fact, it is to the denial of interest that we can most successfully look for interest. In a variation on this theme, Bucket articulates the meaning of the mask of disinterestedness when he says, of Skimpole: "Whenever a person proclaims to you 'In worldly matters I'm a child,' . . . you have got that person's number, and it's Number One" (832). For Bucket, the refusal of knowledge—like the refusal of interest—is just that: a refusal. Rather than signifying the absence of knowledge, it is a strategy for evading the responsibility that attends the ownership of knowledge.[17]

It is through her denegations that readers gain the sense that they know more about Esther than she knows about herself. When Esther says, "As if this narrative were the narrative of *my* life!" or "They said I was so gentle, but I am sure *they* were!", we "emend," as Freud does with his patient: so she *is* the subject. Esther's denegations signal her otherness to herself—the presence of material she wishes to distance herself from—and even as they efface her, they constitute her, marking her for us as a distinctive personality whose most prominent feature is a very loud insistence on her own insignificance. But they also comprise a narrative strategy that enables Esther to construct her identity while—and by—constructing herself as a reflection of the gazes of others. What then is at stake for Esther in the doubleness or denegation of her discourse, the letting in of material she insists she keeps out?

Dickens gives Esther's divided subjectivity a fictional origin and linguistic analogue in her godmother's characterization of Esther's relationship to her mother, which is, for a long time,

17. The relationship between interest and knowledge here is the same as that between pleasure/unpleasure and judgment in Freud's structure. We "know" what we have an interest in; impersonal knowledge is a transformation of personal interest.

all Esther knows of her mother.[18] Mrs. Rachael replies to Esther's question about her origins with these words: "Your mother, Esther, is your disgrace, and you were hers" (65). Her words identify Esther and her mother rhetorically, making them mirror images of one another. Esther immediately reproduces this stucture in connection with the doll to which she confides her troubles: "I was to no one upon earth what Dolly was to me" (65). According to this reflexive and reflective structure, to exist is to exist *for* someone, and to be nothing for someone is therefore to be a blank, an absence. It is as "nothing" that Esther is mirrored even by the doll who is "something" to her, the doll "who used to sit . . . staring at me—or not so much at me, I think, as at nothing" (62). Unseen by her mother, Esther seems to herself to be absent, dead—a recognition she represents symbolically by burying the doll when she departs for Bleak House. At the same time this burial and this sense of herself as absence suggest that she also identifies with her mother as the guilty absence, that she feels herself to be the disgrace reflected by her mother's empty place.

Mrs. Rachael's statement positions Esther ambiguously, as either subject or object. As her mother's disgrace, she is either a separate embodiment of disgrace or an attribute of her mother's. Thus she is, again as Lacan argues of the mirror stage, both reflected by and alienated from her mother's image. And the structure of Mrs. Rachael's statement allows for a play of identification and alienation, or similarity and difference, that enables Esther to structure herself as subject by structuring herself as object, directing the course of her narrative and articulating her own identity while claiming that it is articulated by others.

In Mrs. Rachael's statement, and those statements of Esther's which echo it throughout the novel, identity depends upon the reflexivity of subject and object: "what this lady so

18. Alex Zwerdling writes that "her godmother's words . . . become the most powerful determinant of her adult personality and life choices." See his "Esther Summerson Rehabilitated," *PMLA* 88 (1973): 430.

curiously was to me, I was to her" (372). Such sentences posit no origin; subject and object exist, suspended, only as reflections of one another. Moreover, this structure leaves open the possibility of substitution: "this lady" may be someone other than the mother. And throughout her narrative, Esther replaces the object labeled "disgrace" with good objects, shaping her rhetoric and her narrative so that she will be reflected by good objects rather than bad. Thus, while denying her position as subject, she transforms herself. Through a strategy of self-effacement, merely reporting what she sees in others or what others say about her, she deliberately constructs her own reflection.

She does so because she comes into existence as a subject divided between innocence and guilt, and because the reflective structure of her character—its play of identification and alienation—accommodates both. As soon as she hears Miss Rachael's statement, Esther feels a desire "to repair the fault I had been born with (of which I confessedly felt guilty and yet innocent)" (65). Her goal then becomes "to do some good to some one, and win some love to myself if I could" (65). In other words, Esther's goal is the separation of herself from the bad object—her mother—and from that part of herself which is identified with her mother. And she will accomplish this goal by seeking out love in return for goodness, by substituting good objects for the bad object that is her mother. It is this production of good images which gives us the proliferation of Esther-doubles in the novel—Caddy, Charley, and, most important, Ada. Yet even as Esther transforms the object, and hence herself as subject, the structure of her discourse remains unchanged. Esther's denegations are thus double in more than one way. They both contain and do not contain her mother, and they are an acknowledgment of the guilty self as well as a protestation of innocence, a refusal to make any claim whatsoever. Esther Summerson will be only what others say she is, the object for whom others are subjects. And while her asserted absence from the subject's position displays her continued need to deny what is "other" to her, it also defines her as acted upon rather than acting, an innocent object of the determinations of others.

The rhetorical structure governing Esther's narrative thus strikingly reproduces the way she constructs, or construes, her identity. She is to others what they are to her; she speaks not of herself but of others. She is, as Flaubert said of the novelist (and as I have said of the omniscient narrator), everywhere and nowhere at once. Denegation allows the speaker to have it both ways: to be present and yet absent, letting herself in even as she insists on her desire to keep herself out. Denegation *is* the structure of Esther's identity, a structure "given" to her by others (as the scene with Mrs. Rachael almost allegorically enacts) in the same sense that, according to Lacan, language constitutes the unconscious. For the doubleness of denegation is also the doubleness of language, which both names and refuses to name, structuring the subject even as the positions it articulates—such as "I" and "you"—refer to no one in particular, thus leaving open the possibility of movement and substitution.[19]

Esther comes into existence for herself already structured by what Lacan calls the symbolic: by language, morality, and the law. Feeling herself to be both guilty and innocent, she fashions her narrative to confirm her as the latter but not the former. And the subject-object confusion described above enables her to do so. Though her discourse possesses an imaginary quality in that she seems unable to distinguish herself from those around her, that inability serves her purpose, allowing her to deny the unpleasurable self. At the end of her narrative she has not lost the tendency to see herself reflected everywhere. Rather, she has succeeded in constructing a world which reflects only the self she wishes to see. But that ideal self nevertheless continues to reveal, in the structure of her discourse, what has presumably been expunged from it. Esther's narrative thus reflects the conflict necessitated by the taking of a place within the social world, for, empowered as narrator to construct an identity for herself, she can do so only by choosing one identity and rejecting another. Paradoxically, then, the construction of identity here requires effacement,

19. See Benveniste, "Relations of Person in the Verb," in *Problems of General Linguistics*, pp. 195–204.

the repression of identity. And where David Copperfield's self-effacements reflect his centrality as middle-class male subject, the complexities inherent in Esther's self-construction exemplify the tension between empowerment and disempowerment characteristic of Victorian middle-class femininity. As Jane Gallop observes, "women's traditional place in culture [is] neither subject nor object but disturbingly both. Woman's ambiguous cultural place may be precisely the standpoint from which it is possible to muddle the subject/object distinction."[20] And because for Esther self-construction requires self-effacement, any attempt to align the two narratives with the categories of the personal and the impersonal breaks down. For that difference already exists within her.

The split between the two narratives, as I suggested earlier, might seem easily to be resolved by such a division. Indeed, a distinction between the personal and the impersonal is the one the usual account of first- and third-person requires us to make. The novel further structures the difference between its two narratives as one of limitation and knowledge, and as the difference between "the eye of affection" and "the eye of business" (607), to use the novel's own words. But both narratives blur the distinctions between knowledge that belongs to the self and knowledge that is the property of others. Both narrators "efface" themselves, in different ways and to different degrees, but ultimately for the same purpose: to locate elsewhere, as narrators fantasmatically can, what "belongs" to the self.

The third-person narrative displays the kind of detached, impersonal interest in the secrets of others typical of characters such as Tulkinghorn and Bucket, while Esther, as we know, has a personal reason to feel "interested about my mama" (63). Corresponding to the first narrative's impersonality is the idea of "duty," the impersonal performance of tasks which prompts individuals to neglect such values as friendship and family, and which, John Lucas argues, is at the heart of Dickens's critique of society in this novel: "[M]uch of the

---

20. Jane Gallop, *Reading Lacan* (Ithaca: Cornell University Press, 1985), p. 15.

horror of the social situation that Dickens presents in *Bleak House* is caused by people doing their duty."[21] Strangely, however, the novel presents "duty" as looking very much like the personal. Thus the Bagnets, observing Bucket as, unbeknownst to them, he takes George Rouncewell into custody, remark that Bucket "almost clings to George like, and seems to be really fond of him" (733). And thus Esther, according to Jarndyce, would have sacrificed her love for Woodcourt to "a sense of duty and affection . . . so completely, so entirely, so religiously, that you should never suspect it, though you watched her night and day" (914). Indeed, the terms in which Esther expresses her decision to accompany Bucket on his search for Lady Dedlock fluctuate madly between the personal and the impersonal: "It seemed to become personally important to myself that the truth should be discovered," she says. "In a word, I felt as if it were my duty and obligation to go with them" (759). "Myself," in this sentence, remains strangely distant from the self; it is a third-person self, a self Esther does not seem to know. And feeling is distanced, "about" duty and obligation (*"as if* it were my duty and obligation") rather than their object, which, in any case, is not Lady Dedlock but "myself." Lady Dedlock is the impersonal solution to a mystery which "seems" to concern Esther personally; it is as the location of "truth" that she must be sought out.

Personal knowledge in *Bleak House* can thus be said to take a peculiarly impersonal form. Esther responds to her own personal interests with busyness. After a reference to Woodcourt, she finds herself "humming all the tunes I knew; and . . . working and working in a desperate manner, and I talked and talked, morning, noon, and night" (742). "I had only to be busy and forget it" (561), she says of her lost looks. Talk—what Esther calls "prosing, prosing"—is relief and release, but it is also repression. It is what takes over, as Lady Dedlock fears, when the subject is gone ("Is it the town talk yet?" [632]), and it also participates in doing away with, or reinventing, the subject. The connection between busyness and business tells us much about the relationship between the two

21. Lucas, *The Melancholy Man*, p. 214.

narratives, between "the eye of affection" and "the eye of business." Business, in the third-person narrative, is the name for interest in others' personal affairs; busyness is what Esther turns to when anything that immediately concerns her nears the surface of the text. Esther is "full of business" (173), and she is so, I would argue, because about herself she is "content to know no more" (149). The chief business of English law is, of course, to make business for itself, and that business creates a smooth surface which overlays "the roughness of the suitors' lives and deaths" (399)—the same smooth surface, of course, that covers Tulkinghorn and Bucket.

Esther's narrative, of course, never attains such smoothness; her language always displays itself as a mechanism of repression. She disowns "personal" knowledge: the secret of her birth possesses the peculiar status of being about her—constituting her—and yet never belonging to her. It is free-floating knowledge which others possess for her and which, after Mrs. Rachael's outburst, she does not want to possess. For when Esther finally comes face-to-face with her mother—to take possession, it seems, of her secret—her impulse is to distance herself from her mother and from the secret, as if she were only in the business of keeping the secrets of others. Like Tulkinghorn and Jarndyce, Esther becomes the keeper of someone else's secret, a secret she can keep because she has in fact truly given it away. I have said that Esther's unconscious "speaks" in her denials: what she denies at this point is that "the secret" is hers. "If the secret had been mine," she says, "I must have confided it to Ada. . . . But it was not mine; and I did not feel that I had a right to tell it" (573). To Woodcourt, she says, "I need wish to keep no secret of my own from you; if I keep any, it is another's" (861). Her feeling for Lady Dedlock seems to be primarily one of obligation and duty—"my duty was to bless and receive her" (565)—and the keeping of the secret a duty performed for another: "My present duty appeared to be plain" (573).[22]

---

22. I am not suggesting that Esther should own her mother's secret, but only that she inevitably does. As Gordon Hirsch points out, "[G]uilt and responsibility . . . for [a] parent's sexual vagaries, are not so easily put

The reflexivity of Esther's rhetoric breaks down when she describes her meeting with her mother. Though the two have been identified in a number of ways—by sentences in which subject and object mirror one another, by the scarred face which links Esther to her mother's sexual guilt, and by the wearing of veils—when the two finally meet, Esther denies, and her scarred face enables her to deny, the existence of any resemblance between them.

The scarred face has been recognized by many readers as symbolic of Lady Dedlock's sexual crime.[23] Esther's disfiguration, like David Copperfield's marked face, signals the construction of the self by another: the mark is a metaphor for a character's status as object for a narrator. But Esther's scar has another function. Introducing difference where there had been similarity, it allows her to deny her identification with her mother. After her illness, when Esther observes her face in the mirror, the language of familiarity merges with that of separation: "At first, my face was so strange to me. . . . Very soon it became more familiar, and then I knew the extent of the alteration in it better than I had done at first" (559). And when Lady Dedlock reveals herself to Esther, Esther responds

---

aside. . . . Esther, once acknowledged as Lady Dedlock's illegitimate daughter, would not so easily escape from the social consequences of the sins of her parents, regardless of how innocent she may feel herself to be." See "The Mysteries in *Bleak House*: A Psychoanalytic Study," *Dickens Studies Annual* 4 (1975): 137.

Karen Chase discusses Esther's use of personal pronouns, as well as the shift from "my" to "the" that occurs between Lady Dedlock and Tulkinghorn in chapter 48. ("It is no longer your secret," says Tulkinghorn.) Chase's general point is that the third-person narrative is characterized by the impersonal form and Esther's by the personal. For instance, she cites the change from "the mother of the dead child" to "it was my mother, cold and dead" when Esther and Bucket discover Lady Dedlock's body. Yet she does not discuss Esther's use of impersonal forms, and it would also seem important to note that Esther can acknowledge her relationship to her mother only in the past tense: "It *was* my mother." See *Eros and Psyche* (New York: Methuen, 1984), pp. 115–17.

23. Christine Van Boheemen-Saaf writes that Esther's disease "is on a symbolic level related to the unbridled sexuality of Esther's parents; and 'smallpox' is indeed close enough to 'pox' to assume a sexual connotation": "The Universe Makes an Indifferent Parent," in Joseph H. Smith and William Kerrigan, eds., *Interpreting Lacan* (New Haven: Yale University Press, 1983), p. 245.

with an astounding expression of her need to differentiate herself from the figure she most resembles:

> I felt, through all my tumult of emotion, a burst of gratitude to the providence of God that I was so changed as that I never could disgrace her by any trace of likeness; as that nobody could ever now look at me, and look at her, and remotely think of any near tie between us. (565)

Here, as in Mrs. Rachael's statement, the question of who disgraces whom remains ambiguous; the "tie" reveals each to be potentially the other's disgrace. Esther's disfiguration and the veil that covers it signal her ambivalent status as both character and narrator, at once like and unlike her mother. As character, she shares her mother's "disfigurement"; as narrator, she has the power to efface it, shifting the scar's significance solely to her mother. (And it is significant that her scarred face—like her unscarred face—is never really described. We as readers never "see" Esther.)

As the novel progresses, Esther's narrative, in conjunction with the impersonal detectives of the third-person narrative, externalizes and displaces the secret of Esther's origin, the plot underscoring this conjunction when she joins Bucket in pursuit of Lady Dedlock.[24] The "other" narrative's impersonal approach to Lady Dedlock's secret may make the revelation of the secret seem "impersonal and inevitable," as John Frazee writes, but Esther's narrative finally does the same.[25] Esther's personal history is ultimately defined only as her mother's secret; where she had looked for likeness she is now grateful to perceive difference. And this is not simply a refusal to recognize whatever similarity might exist between her mother and herself, a refusal we might locate at an unconscious level. Esther's narrative is constructed so that, when she and her mother finally meet, recognition is in fact problematic because

---

24. This collapse is represented in Dickens's number plans for the novel by the phrase "Mr. Bucket and Esther." See the Penguin edition of *Bleak House*, p. 950.

25. John P. Frazee, "The Character of Esther and the Narrative Structure of *Bleak House*," *Studies in the Novel* 17 (1985): 235.

likeness has actually been erased. Denial thus takes place not just at an unconscious level within the narrative, but is built into the narrative's structure. After Esther's illness, her very appearance constitutes a denial of her mother. Indeed, we might say that this is the very function of her illness. If Esther feels "guilty and yet innocent," the structure of her narrative allows her to do so, enabling her to differentiate herself from the bad object while not assigning to her the responsibility for doing so.

Esther's initial response to her meeting with her mother is the sense that "the blame and shame were all in me" (570). But she soon asserts her innocence in a way that she has been unable to throughout her entire narrative: "I knew I was as innocent of my birth as a queen of hers; and that before my Heavenly Father I should not be punished for birth, nor a queen rewarded for it" (571). The discovery of her parentage is at once a realization and a terrible unrealization of the family romance. Esther discovers that she is of noble parentage only to find that her mother's nobility is damaged beyond repair. Associating her own birth with that of royalty, she finds herself blameless, and is able to do so, it seems, because the "blame and shame" have found their proper object.

Esther's relationship to her mother evokes a fear of the loss of distinctions similar to Sir Leicester's anxiety about the loss of distinctions between social classes—his fear that "the flood-gates of society are burst open" (628). In fact, the novel's famed emphasis on connection between social classes fails entirely when it comes to Esther's relationship with her mother. The novel achieves social coherence not by inclusiveness but through the elimination of difference; Esther comes into her own as a member of the social structure, and of a family, by eliminating the image in which she did not want to see herself reflected.

Responsibility has long been considered a major theme of *Bleak House*, but the novel's structure, in which a subject presents herself as object, makes it difficult to connect knowledge and responsibility at the level of narrative. The end of Esther's narrative stresses "sameness," asserting the persistence of the conditions that preceded Lady Dedlock's irruption into the placid life of Bleak House. Jarndyce is "what he has ever been"; Esther keeps "all her old names" and her seat in the chair by his side, "just the same" (934). Her true origins revealed and thereby, it seems, expunged, Esther is installed in a family she has found on her own. And just as the end of her narrative reinforces her continued dependence on others for a view of herself ("The people even praise Me as the doctor's wife. . . . They like Me for his sake, as I do everything I do in life for his sake" [935]), so too does it continue to obscure the extent to which she plays a role in the construction of her narrative—or, what is the same thing, in the determination of those who will surround her at its end. Nowhere does the novel say, for instance, that Esther "passively colludes" with Bucket to pursue Lady Dedlock to her death.[26] And yet it says so everywhere in the language of denegation, which would kill the mother by denial—in the dreamlike recognition scene, for instance, in which Esther essentially claims, "It was *not* my mother." As in the structure of denegation itself, at the end of Esther's narrative we are caught between intellect and affect, or consciousness and unconsciousness: between seeing Esther as she sees herself—as an object of the gazes of others, merely reporting what they say about her—and acknowledging that she has played some role in the construction of those gazes, and hence of her own identity.

Constituting as it does a subject who does not know herself, denegation may be seen as integral to the fiction of Esther's consciousness—the fiction that Esther *is* a consciousness. By means of denegation, a subject presumed not to know can in fact know, and can relay to readers what they need to know without seeming to be a mere mouthpiece for the author, without ever seeming "out of character." Thus Esther can chastise Skimpole as long as she seems in awe of

---

26. These are Virginia Blain's words: "Double Vision and the Double Standard in *Bleak House*: A Feminist Perspective," in Harold Bloom, ed., *Modern Critical Interpretations: Bleak House* (New York: Chelsea House, 1987), p. 155.

him; she can suggest that she distrusts Richard because she at the same time announces her distrust of herself for doing so.[27] Presenting herself as alienated from her own knowledge, Esther cannot be held responsible for what she knows or says. Her denials are essential to the sense we have of her as a passive construction, a character who is not responsible for what she knows. Similarly, knowledge in the third-person narrative emanates from no specific source. Seeing is done by objects: "Mirrors reflect" (210), "fire watches" (78), the house "stares" (817), and the sunshine "looks" (203), as does the "wintry morning" (418). A view of Lady Dedlock comes, ventriloquistically, from "authorities of "the world of fashion" (57). Indeed, of the "conductor" of the opinions dispersed throughout the third-person narrative, we might say what the narrator himself says of the Lord Chancellor's "very little counsel": "Everybody looks for him. Nobody can see him" (54). Thus while *Bleak House* makes responsibility one of its central thematic issues, that same issue is, at the level of narration, the novel's essentially unsolvable (and unspeakable) problem. In its two narratives, the novel asserts the impossibility of fixing responsibility for knowledge. It is a structure that, to quote the words of that sinister but perspicacious character Vholes once again, "divides the responsibility of knowing."

Reporting what he knows of Richard's troubled situation in order to divide this responsibility, Vholes acts, he says, in neither his personal nor his professional capacity: he wants specifically to do something which "can be charged to nobody" (672). Between the personal and the impersonal resides "nobody." And it is between Esther's unspeakable personal desire to separate herself from her mother, and the professional duty which has the novel's detectives seeking her out, that Lady Dedlock's death takes place—a death that, serving personal and impersonal interests, is also chargeable to no-

---

27. Suzanne Graver discusses Esther's inability to reconcile her critical sense with the Victorian womanly ideal in "Writing in a 'Womanly' Way and the Double Vision of *Bleak House*," *Dickens Quarterly* 4 (1987): 3–14.

body. Just as the novel divides the responsibility of knowing between its two narratives, so too is knowledge divided within individual subjects, in what we commonly understand to be the division between consciousness and unconsciousness. And if the responsibility of knowing is divided, where are we to locate the subject who knows?

It is tempting—and many critics have been tempted—to make Esther the source of *Bleak House*'s general anxiety about knowledge. Indeed, it is tempting precisely because the novel offers us Esther's personal history, I would argue, as an answer to the omniscient narrative's obsessive concern with knowledge and secrecy. Esther's story provides a source for the omniscient narrative's anxiety about knowledge; indeed, we might say that her narrative in fact exists in order to do so. For as psychoanalytic criticism of the novel has demonstrated, the omniscient narration's obsession with secrecy and anxiety about knowledge may be traced to the blocking of Esther's curiosity about her mother.[28] Unlike Tulkinghorn and Bucket, that is, Esther has a personal reason for being interested in her mother: "I had never heard of my papa either, but I felt more interested about my mama" (63). In another birthday scene imbued with feelings of emptiness and alienation, of something missing at the center, Esther's sense both of her difference from others and of her similarity to her mother is reinforced by the striking reciprocity of Mrs. Rachael's comment. Since Esther's curiosity is met with this explosion of wrath and a warning about disgrace, Esther understands only that it is dangerous to ask about her origins and might be still more dangerous to receive an answer. And she substitutes for the knowledge she cannot get incessant talk about her inability to find out, as well as a sense of herself as full of secrets: "[H]ow often I repeated to the doll the story of my birthday" (65).

---

28. As Gordon Hirsch writes, "*Bleak House* deserves to be considered one of Dickens's first achievements precisely because its formal design as a mystery so successfully expresses and attempts to work through its latent content, its concern with the investigation of the mysteries associated with parental sexuality." "The Mysteries in *Bleak House*," p. 152.

I busily stitched away, and told her every one of my secrets.
. . . It almost makes me cry to think what a relief it used to be
to me, when I came home from school of a day, to run upstairs
to my room, and say, 'O you dear faithful Dolly, I knew you
would be expecting me!' and then to sit down on the floor . . .
and tell her all I had noticed since we parted. (62)

Esther's world becomes full of secrets she is forbidden to
investigate, and her "noticing way," a response to this, may be
seen as the source of the unmotivated curiosity that many of
the novel's characters manifest.

Esther's personal history, in other words, can stand as the
source for the other narrative's anxieties about knowledge.
But if we argue that her history performs this function, can we
not also see the situation in reverse? That is, if we regard the
subject's case history as the source of a more diffuse anxiety
about knowledge, might we not also consider that anxiety to
be the source of what appears in the novel as the subject—as
"case history" or individual psychology? Esther's story "contains" the anxiety about knowledge that the other narrative
displays; as personal history, her secret can be known, contained, expunged. But if an answer to supposedly objective
conditions can be localized in the individual subject, it is also
the case that the subject has been constructed to serve precisely that function: to fall ill and be cured, in a process that
keeps society from seeing itself as needing curing. For just as
Esther's narrative may be said to provide an origin for the
concerns of the novel as a whole, so too does the novel's
"Other" produce the subject as an effect of its concerns: "The
consistent subject is the place to which the representations of
ideology are directed: Duty, Morality, and Law all depend on
this category of subject for their functioning, and all contribute
as institutions to its production."[29] Each voice is what the
other is not. Esther may be said to derive from, or to be the

29. Rosalind Coward and John Ellis, *Language and Materialism* (London:
Routledge and Kegan Paul, 1977), p. 76. See also Alan Sheridan's "Translator's
Note," in *Ecrits*: "the subject, in Lacan's sense, is himself an effect of the
symbolic" (ix).

effect of, the "Other" narrative, just as it may be said to derive from her.

The subject lives, as Rosemary Coward and John Ellis put it, an "imaginary wholeness": "Ideologies set in place the individual as though he were this subject: the individual produces himself in this imaginary wholeness, this imaginary reflection of himself as the author of his actions" (76). In the reading presented here, the imaginary quality of Esther's narrative becomes visible. Her narrative positions her within the social whole, but the structure of her narrative reveals that her position depends on a denial of difference. Omniscience is similarly, as I have been arguing, an imaginary wholeness—one whose imaginary quality is more difficult to perceive because it typically provides us no place to stand outside it. In *Bleak House*, however, it does provide us with such a place, not only in what is offered as the subject's personal history but also in the space between the two narratives, suggesting thereby the other perspectives we have not been offered as well as the way each narrative derives its significance from the other. Rather than seeing omniscience merely as an effect or derivation of individual psychology, then, we can say that omniscience gains its power from the very notion of individual psychology, which it constructs and on which it depends. Omniscience and first-person exist only as reflexes of one another. We can thus use the opportunity afforded by the novel's double narration to do what omniscience cannot do: to stand in the space between what is constructed as the subject and the impersonal agency which seems to construct it. The imaginary wholeness of each will appear imaginary only from such a position.

David Copperfield's and Esther Summerson's narratives illustrate that the construction of the social subject paradoxically requires self-effacement—that as some aspects of identity are constructed and confirmed through narrative, others must be disavowed. But the difference in gender of these two narrators has consequences for the form and substance of their construction. In both novels Dickens balances self-effacement against what is, in cultural terms, self-fulfillment.

And yet differences between David's and Esther's characteristic evasions of knowledge and responsibility are registered in the success with which each conveys an effect or illusion of fulfillment, in the extent to which, we might say, self-effacement is concealed by self-inscription. Where David consciously assumes his position as narrator and progresses toward the full assumption of his father's name, Esther ends as "the doctor's wife," all the while insisting upon her tangential status. Where the construction of the social self always requires denial, the Victorian angelic ideal takes denial as its principle, making even a fiction of fulfillment difficult to maintain.

Both narratives trace a movement from an apprehension of the self as "nobody" to the occupying of a position as "somebody," and in both cases that movement entails loss as well as gain: for Esther, the loss of the self identified with Lady Dedlock; for David, the sacrifice of numerous characters with whom the narrator refuses to acknowledge his identification. As characters, both come into existence as scars, or marks; as narrators, both work to efface this markedness. In doing so, however, they reveal the way they are ineluctably shaped by the linguistic and cultural systems they inhabit.

❨ 5 ❩

Our Mutual Friend
On Taking the Reader by Surprise

Our Mutual Friend is generally regarded as the most modern of Dickens's works because of the absence of a prominent omniscient voice and a clear omniscient perspective—the kind of voice and perspective we are told we find in earlier novels such as *Bleak House* and *Little Dorrit*. Presumably, in *Our Mutual Friend*, one never knows exactly where the novelist stands because he always stands partly inside his characters. As J. Hillis Miller has put it, "he can only see the world [of the novel] as it appears from the perspective of some particular personage or group of personages who are not, as he is, mere spectators, but are actively engaged in the world."[1] Without such an external view, connections remain unstated and problems unresolved, resulting in the fragmentation and confusion which have earned for the novel the name "modern."

Yet as we have seen, if the Dickens narrator lets his omniscience go without saying, he by no means lets it go without being felt. Here, as everywhere in Dickens, omniscience is an active force which makes characters and readers aware of its presence. It is precisely the sense of being "inside" character—encouraging in readers an illusion of being "inside"—that allows the narrator of *Our Mutual Friend* to demonstrate his omniscience.

---

1. J. Hillis Miller, *Charles Dickens: The World of His Novels* (Cambridge: Harvard University Press, 1958), p. 292. See also Ermarth's idea of omniscience as "collective consciousness" in *Realism and Consensus in the English Novel*.

The problematic of omniscience as surprise in *Our Mutual Friend* is foregrounded in *Bleak House*. One of the peculiarities of Esther Summerson's narratorial role, as we saw in the previous chapter, is that her narrative always knows more than she does. Readers are provided with clues enabling them to understand more than they could from the information she provides, or professes to be aware of. What Esther says, that is, often matters less than the fact that she talks a great deal, or blushes, or claims to have nothing to say. When Jarndyce suggests retaining Mrs. Woodcourt at Bleak House, for example, Esther feels uneasy, but refuses to investigate the source of her feeling: "I had nothing to say," she says. "At least I had nothing in my mind that I could say. I had an undefined impression that it might have been better if we had had some other inmate, but I could hardly have explained why, even to myself" (871). The reader, of course, could easily offer an explanation. Although we might expect a first-person narrative to create in the reader a sense of affinity or identity with its speaker, Esther's narrative encourages a sense of omniscience with respect to her. Readers pursue a system of signs that define Esther as a character who does not know herself, even at the very end of her narrative, when all she knows has presumably been revealed.

What seems to be a deliberate pitting of one level of knowledge against another occurs elsewhere in the novel, as various characters demonstrate to one another their possession of knowledge. In one scene, for example, Tulkinghorn, who knows Lady Dedlock's history, tells what he knows to an audience consisting of Lady Dedlock, Sir Leicester, and Cousin Volumnia. The subject of the story, however, remains anonymous.

> [T]his lady preserved a secret under all her greatness, which she had preserved for many years. . . . a train of circumstances with which I need not trouble you, led to discovery. As I received the story, they began in an imprudence on her part one day, when she was taken by surprise; which shows how difficult it is for the firmest of us (she was very firm) to be always guarded. (629)

Tulkinghorn's purpose in relating his narrative in this way is to let Lady Dedlock know that he knows her story. Like many other moments in *Bleak House*, it reveals more than it explicitly tells, relying on readers' and listeners' knowledge to supplement its meaning. The scene provides two distinct possibilities for readerly identification. While sharing in Tulkinghorn's knowledge, we also participate in Lady Dedlock's sudden apprehension of being discovered. This combination of knowledge and lack of knowledge manifests itself over and over again in *Bleak House*, most obviously, as I have shown, in the novel's narrative structure, which similarly divides readerly identification.

Lady Dedlock's "start" visibly manifests both knowledge and a failure of knowledge: by revealing that she knows something, she endangers what she knows. The rupture in her typically bored demeanor makes her vulnerable to the lawyer's gaze; the visible sign—her movement or expression of surprise—reveals depth where there had previously been only surface. The novel stresses the implacability of those characters exceptional for the knowledge they possess. There is never "a ruffle on the surface" of Tulkinghorn's "unfathomable depths" (363); Bucket can "dip down to the bottom of his mind" (362) while his expression remains unchanged. Bucket's implacability is in fact defined as his ability not to be surprised: "There's not a move on the board that would surprise me" (782), he claims. In the rhetoric of Dickensian character, then, surprise—the capacity to be surprised—is a measure of permeability and vulnerability.

The "earlier imprudence" to which Tulkinghorn refers is another moment at which Lady Dedlock was taken by surprise: that moment at which she catches a glimpse of a law clerk's familiar handwriting, thus alerting the lawyer (sensitive to every movement) to the existence of a mystery—signalling the existence of something he doesn't know. As Tulkinghorn's narrative points out, this is in a sense the novel's originating moment, the moment which prompts the uncovering of Lady Dedlock's history. Surprise operates as both beginning and ending, provoking the opening up of a dormant past, the reinterpretation of an already established narrative in the context of a new ending. To begin a novel with a moment of surprise is to begin what must be a retrospective account, a retracing of the past in terms of that moment. To end a novel with one, especially as complete a surprise as Dickens engineers for *Our Mutual Friend*, is also to require a turning back, or peripety, engendering in the reader a double sense of the text and of him or herself.

The moment of surprise doubles and reverses the self, producing a self that knows and a self that only thought it knew. There are several possible accounts of this effect. On the one hand, we have the idea that surprise provides a moment of recognition and hence a pleasant experience: "True enough! And I never thought of it," goes one translation of Aristotle's *Rhetoric*. "When we see the veiled meaning, we are conscious of our success in learning."[2] Robert Caserio, however, cites Aristotle as implying, by peripety, "the terrible, untrustworthy mutability of experience," but proceeds to argue that sense of instability away, declaring that surprise finally reassures us: "[R]ecognition scenes in Dickens make the reader grasp the unity and relatedness of all human experience."[3]

The preceding quotations suggest that surprise always provides a satisfying recognition, a reawakening of knowledge already possessed. And Tulkinghorn's narrative does call Lady Dedlock's attention to her own history. But these discussions fail to consider the sense of exposure and vulnerability that accompanies Lady Dedlock's discovery that she has been discovered. Surprise here involves not only a recognition of previous knowledge but the opening up of a danger zone: an awareness that her personal history has become the property of others.

Caserio connects the characters' experience of surprise to that of the readers: Dickens's "plots create recognition scenes

2. Lane Cooper, ed., *The Rhetoric of Aristotle* (New Jersey: Prentice-Hall, 1960), pp. 212–13.

3. Robert Caserio, *Plot, Story, and the Novel* (New Jersey: Princeton University Press, 1983), p. 57.

for the reader that are only secondarily the discovery of the literal relations among persons in the story" (72). To the extent that a reader expects, somewhere during the course of a novel, the solution to a mystery, Caserio seems correct. Surprise at the solution may be experienced as recognition, and may be pleasant or satisfying. But if the reader, like Lady Dedlock, is not expecting to be surprised—is not even aware, like the reader of *Our Mutual Friend*, that there is a mystery to be solved—then surprise operates in a much less reassuring manner: as the novel's exposure of vulnerability and lack of knowledge in its readers. Peripety is first destabilizing, and only later reassuring, once the reader—the object of surprise—has had the opportunity to reconstruct the narrative, recasting the moment of surprise as its proper ending.

In my reading of *The Old Curiosity Shop*, I pointed to a series of scenes in which characters suddenly become aware of an observer's presence. Each moment of surprise marks a displacement of narratorial power, a shift in narratorial position. Each moment, I noted, has a distancing effect on the reader, who is moved from presumably unselfconscious involvement in a scene to a position framing that scene. That movement in turn reveals the possibility of reversibility on which, I have argued, narrator-character relationships in Dickens are based. As a result of this shift, the reader, previously involved only with the focal character, experiences an immediate awareness of his or her observational limitations. While identification, then—the movement of sympathy—can give the reader narratorial insight, it can also make him or her vulnerable to the same failures of vision that accompany the character's position. Inherent in these moments of surprise, then, is a principle of reversibility: the reversibility of "I" and "you." And this alteration in the reader's position betrays the narrator's awareness of his own potential vulnerability.

Often, as in *Bleak House*, such surprises do not bear directly on a novel's plot. A narrator or character simply seems to take pleasure in the ability to control a flow of information, measuring that ability by the force of the shock produced. Narrative in *Bleak House* is frequently used by one character to surprise and upset another. Bucket tells the story of his "beautiful case" to Sir Leicester, saying "a gentleman can bear a shock, when it must come, boldly and steadily" (781); at the end of the narrative, as we know, Sir Leicester collapses. And when Jarndyce reveals to Esther his plot to marry her to Woodcourt, he engages her in a competition for knowledge which seems at odds with the confidence that supposedly exists between them. Having earlier possessed and then revealed Esther's personal history to her, Jarndyce now constructs a personal history for her. Taking her to see the new Bleak House, he pretends that it is meant for Woodcourt alone. And as Esther begins to laugh and cry, Jarndyce makes light of her assertion that she has known all along.

> "Well, well," said he, "I am delighted that you approve. I thought you would. I meant it as a pleasant surprise for the little mistress of Bleak House."
> I kissed him, and dried my eyes. "I know now!" said I. "I have seen this in your face a long while."
> "No; have you really, my dear?" said he. "What a Dame Durden it is to read a face!" (911)

Esther has, of course, misread Jarndyce's face all along, as has the reader, who shares her surprise. And Jarndyce's explanation for withholding the plot is simply a narrator's pleasure in keeping a secret: "When Allan Woodcourt spoke to you, my dear, he spoke with my knowledge and consent—but I gave him no encouragement, not I, for these surprises were my great reward, and I was too miserly to part with a scrap of it" (914).[4]

In both examples, the telling of narrative is aesthetically pleasing for the teller but at the same time unleashes more hostile force than circumstances would seem to warrant. In both, narrative appears to be a form of action, albeit a weak one.[5] The title of the Bucket chapter is, appropriately, "Spring-

---

4. Jarndyce here resembles Tulkinghorn, whose "calling is the acquisition of secrets, and the holding possession of such power as they give him" (567).

5. On narrative as action, see A. J. Greimas and J. Courtes, "The Cognitive Dimension of Narrative Discourse," *New Literary History* 7 (1976): 433–47.

ing a Mine." Using a violent metaphor, Dickens acknowledges the violence implicit in the act of revelation: surprise as a demonstration of power or force. At least one critic has noted class antagonism in Bucket's destructive storytelling ("a gentleman can bear a shock").[6] And what Jarndyce is really being miserly about, we might argue, is the time left during which he and Esther are, at least at the level of fantasy (his fantasy), intended for one another. Taking her by surprise, he takes her at the same time that he gives her up.

If narrative in these texts is a form of action, knowledge is its object. In *Our Mutual Friend*, the concealment and revelation of knowledge—often knowledge invented solely for the purpose of possessing something no one else possesses—frequently constitutes the characters' main activity. Of John Harmon, alias John Rokesmith, employed as Boffin's secretary, Dickens writes:

> [T]he Secretary was discerning, discreet, and silent, though as zealous as if the affairs [Boffin's] had been his own. He showed no love of patronage or the command of money, but distinctly preferred resigning both to Mr. Boffin. If, in his limited sphere, he sought power, it was the power of knowledge; the power derivable from a perfect comprehension of his business. (241)

But to whom, we might wonder, does that last "his" refer? Harmon's chief activity is narratorial. In disguise, taken into the Wilfer and Boffin households, he succeeds in acquiring knowledge and thereby taking in other characters. And while he is ostensibly collecting knowledge toward some end—the evaluation of Bella Wilfer's character—for most characters in the novel the pursuit of knowledge serves no purpose other than deception. The desire to hide something, to engineer a surprise, is throughout the novel stronger and more significant than the content of the surprise. (We might simply consider the weakness of the novel's central notion, the testing of Bella Wilfer.) Surprises take on a life of their own, diverging

---

6. P. J. M. Scott, *Reality and Comic Confidence in the Novels of Charles Dickens* (London: Macmillan, 1979), p. 71.

from the requirements of plot.[7] And knowledge serves no practical function and has no special power, unless power is defined as the creation of a perceptible gap between one character's knowledge and another's, a gap measured, finally, by its potential to surprise.

The frequent use of disguise and deception in the novel substantiates what we already know about the Dickens narrator: that he has not disappeared so much as gone into hiding. While J. Hillis Miller asserts that the novel never gives an unqualified "inside" view, Bakhtin's discussion of the relation between narratorial and characterological voices in *Little Dorrit* asserts the impossibility of firmly separating the two. "Another's speech," Bakhtin writes, "whether as storytelling, as mimicking, as the display of a thing in light of a particular point of view . . . is at none of these points clearly separated from authorial speech: the boundaries are deliberately flexible and ambiguous."[8] Yet as if to counter this idea of the inseparability of narrator and character, *Our Mutual Friend* traces a pattern of epistemological one-upmanship. Characters not only busy themselves finding out all they can about one another, but they invent their own plots, entrapping others in schemes the point of which is often merely to entrap. It is not that there is one body of knowledge that each character can only know partially, as other accounts of omniscience would have it. Rather, plots do not exist until a character invents them, and they can be invented and put into practice at any time. Knowledge thus exists only by invention, so that no character and no narrator can ever be certain of possessing it in its entirety. It is, therefore, something every character is appropriately anxious about. For one character's plotting leads to

7. Jonathan Arac distinguishes surprises, by definition, from plot: "[S]uch a shock . . . has only symbolic bearing on the action because it surprises us. Inevitability is the characteristic of plot in the sense that I am using the term. The plot is the ground from which the book's events spring and in which their roots can be traced": *Commissioned Spirits*, p. 164.

8. M. M. Bakhtin, "Discourse in the Novel," in *The Dialogic Imagination: Four Essays*, ed. Michael Holquist, trans. Caryl Emerson and Michael Holquist (Austin: University of Texas Press, 1981), p. 308.

another's in a potentially endless reciprocity. As the Lammles say, "we owe all other people the grudge of wishing them to be taken in, as we ourselves have been taken in" (173).

In short, in this novel supposedly wonderful for the relativity of its truths, for the absence of a fixed center or omniscient overseer, each character is anxiously striving to be the director of his own plot, the omniscient narrator of his own fiction—the possessor of knowledge he has invented yet can require other characters to know. The easily identifiable omniscient voice may have disappeared, but concern with omniscience has not. Though we may not be able to locate it in a single, unifying point of view, we cannot miss it in the narrative's structure or in the force of the surprise Dickens engineers for his readers. "Taking in" is thus a narrative project as well as a thematic one. Indeed, it blurs the distinction between theme and structure, narrator and character, in what, borrowing a phrase from Paul de Man, we might call a "rhetorical strategy . . . hidden behind the seductive powers of identification."[9] To be taken in, according to *Our Mutual Friend*, is to become a participant in someone else's plot, the object of someone else's agency, and the target of the narrator's inevitable assertion of omniscience. It is, in short, to be something like a character in a Dickens novel.

Our Mutual Friend keeps its readers on the narratorial side of things, aware of disguises and deceptions as they occur. Taken behind the scenes, the reader sees what "nobody" sees.

> Charming to see Mr. and Mrs. Lammle taking leave so gracefully, and going down the stairs so lovingly and sweetly. Not quite so charming to see their smiling faces fall and brood as they dropped moodily into separate corners of their little carriage. But to be sure that was a sight behind the scenes, which nobody saw, and which nobody was meant to see. (189)

While refusing a single, distinct external perspective, the novel remains obsessively concerned with insides and outsides, and its logic of uncovering the hidden—in the river, the

9. Paul de Man, *Allegories of Reading* (New Haven: Yale University Press, 1979), p. ix.

dustheaps, or the Lammles' carriage—leads the reader to believe in distinctions between deceitful surfaces and underlying truths. Readers know how the Veneerings deceive the Lammles, and the Lammles Georgina; we hear Fledgby and the Lammles plan their trickery. We know, or so we are led to believe, what lies behind the "disinterested" surface: that of the secretary, the servant, the Inspector who "mustn't look like business" (206). But it is knowledge of John Harmon's plotting in particular that convinces readers of the novel's shared omniscience.

The novel provides both negative and positive versions of the Asmodean figure. Silas Wegg, for instance, has a fantasy of knowledge and possession about the house on the corner—"Our House," he calls it—inventing for his own satisfaction its fixtures and inhabitants. But the novel never deceives us about the status of Wegg's fantasies. He is properly disappointed, when allowed to enter the house, at its failure to meet his expectations. And Wegg's attitude toward Boffin displays the same falsely grounded sense of knowledge and power.

> Silas Wegg felt it to be quite out of the question that he could lay his head upon his pillow in peace, without first hovering over Mr. Boffin's house in the superior character of its Evil Genius. Power . . . has ever the greatest attraction for the lowest natures; and the mere defiance of the unconscious house-front, with his power to strip the roof off the inhabiting family like the roof of a house of cards, was a treat which had a charm for Silas Wegg. (564)

In the novel's terms, the ability to interpret houses correctly, and to get inside them, is analogous to the ability to find one's way behind the facade of character, gaining access to the truth behind surfaces. As Wegg notes bitterly, Boffin's preference for Rokesmith over himself as a confidential servant is marked by Rokesmith's free access to the house: "[T]he house is as free to him as if it was his. . . . I am banished to the Bower" (353).

If Wegg is the negative version of the omniscient fantasy, his speculations exposed as mere speculation, Harmon represents the unproblematic, unquestioned embodiment of that fantasy. Inventing and surviving his own fictitious death, he remains present yet invisible, observing and judging, hearing himself spoken about as he plots his life. And nowhere does the novel suggest that there is anything fantastic about this scenario. As "the man from Somewhere," Harmon can choose any identity he likes, and the one he chooses enables him to move freely between establishments, getting to know other people's business without revealing his own. A character who is also an agent of narrative, whose business it is to conceal his own interests in his interest in others, Harmon is a direct descendant of Boz, Humphrey, and the Uncommercial Traveller.

Harmon's experience of the attack on George Radfoot, who is dressed in Harmon's clothes, is one of negative capability—a loss of self in the imagining of the other—analogous to the novelist's imagining of character. If the omniscient fantasy is a fantasy of taking a position outside the self, Harmon achieves it here by identifying the other as himself, transcending his own boundaries by imagining himself dead. But this moment also dramatizes the imaginist's inability to absent himself from his own creation, even after creating a second self in character. Harmon finds himself unable to construct the narrative of his death without "using the word I," even though, as he says, "there was no such thing as I, within my knowledge" (426). At the moment of its own disappearance, then, the self remains to witness the death of what, once detached, becomes another self. As Garrett Stewart writes, death in the novel is always death by displacement, the death of the other.[10]

But most significant about Harmon's extended interior monologue is the sense of transcending boundaries it conveys, the way it seems to extend the experience of omniscience to the reader. There is no deeper level of character than thought itself, particularly the thoughts of a character exploring the dimensions of character, deciding, in effect, what char-

---

10. Garrett Stewart, *Death Sentences* (Cambridge: Harvard University Press, 1984), pp. 17, 19: "a death by displacement—by which I am suggesting a death undergone by proxy so that it can be overseen by a surviving protagonist—that serves to defray the psychic expenditure of an equivalent fatality in the onlooking consciousness"; "death from the security of aesthetic distance."

acter to be—for then the reader is seemingly in on the shaping of the novel itself. Dickens thus uses the character of John Harmon to create the illusion that the reader participates in the very formation of character and plot. And throughout the novel, the act of reading about fantasies of omniscience— Wegg's, Fledgeby's, Harmon's—subtly but inevitably invites the reader to assume that he or she is *not* fantasizing. In order to perceive another's fantasy, one must, after all, be outside of it oneself.

Of Pickwick's innocence and gullibility, G. K. Chesterton has written: "To be taken in everywhere is to see the inside of everything."[11] The reader privileged to be taken behind the scenes of *Our Mutual Friend* is taken in in another sense as well. I refer, of course, to Boffin's supposed transformation: the miserliness which has actually been a pretense intended to demonstrate to Bella Wilfer the evils of loving money. Like Fledgeby, Harmon, and the Lammles, Boffin speaks confidentiality to the reader. Unlike them, however, he remains in disguise while doing so.

> "Now, I wonder," he meditated as he went along, nursing his stick, "whether it can be, that Venus is setting himself to get the better of Wegg? Whether it can be, that he means, when I have bought Wegg out, to have me all to himself and to pick me clean to the bones!"
>
> It was a cunning and suspicious idea, quite in the way of his school of Misers, and he looked very cunning and suspicious as he went jogging through the streets. More than once or twice, more than twice or thrice, say half a dozen times, he took his stick from the arm on which he nursed it, and hit a straight sharp rap at the air with its head. Possibly the wooden countenance of Mr. Silas Wegg was incorporeally before him at those moments, for he hit with intense satisfaction. (650)

The words "looked" and "possibly" might allow us to perceive Boffin's deception; certainly we can see this in retrospect.[12]

---

11. G. K. Chesterton, "*The Pickwick Papers*," in George H. Ford and Lauriat Lane, Jr., eds., *The Dickens Critics* (Ithaca: Cornell University Press, 1966), p. 121.

12. See Rosemary Mundhenk, "The Education of the Reader in *Our Mutual Friend*," *Nineteenth Century Fiction* 34 (1979): 48.

But finally the question of how well the deception is hidden matters less than the idea of using character itself as a trap, as Dickens does throughout the novel. Indeed, having Boffin read books about misers, Dickens relies on the idea of readerly identification as a further means of taking his readers in.

"The reader . . . yearns for a friendly narrator to order his experience," writes U. C. Knoepflmacher; "he feels threatened by a novelist who may be his and the characters' mutual enemy." Knoepflmacher finally claims, however, that surprise makes us feel good: "When Boffin reveals that his 'change' was feigned, that he has actually been 'playing a part,' we are elated. . . . Our security is restored."[13] On the contrary, and as I have been suggesting, it is precisely at the moment of surprise, when we become aware of how misled we have been, that we glimpse the potential depth of our insecurity: the possible existence, always, of knowledge we haven't got. *Our Mutual Friend* depends upon and encourages a sense of omniscience in those it means to surprise. Those plotted against remain ignorant of plots, while in general readers are in on the plotting. Yet when Fledgeby states his purpose as "to work a lot of power over you and you not know it, knowing as you think yourselves" (492), his "you" describes the reader as well, for what is hidden from readers is not simply the solution to a mystery but the existence of one, and the established triadic structure—plotter, victim, and eavesdropping reader—keeps readers thinking they know. Revelation, then, comes with a double force, the force not just of a solution but of one's own epistemological limitations—of having completely and seriously misread. As Wegg says to Venus, "If you was to have a sap-ur-ize, it should be a complete one!" (556).

Part of the difficulty readers have with Boffin's deception lies, I would argue, in the novel's use of deception for both good and bad ends. To deceive is to be a "mutual friend," a morally ambiguous creature. To be everyone's friend, as Twemlow discovers early in the book, is to be no one's in

---

13. U.C. Knoepflmacher, *Laughter and Despair* (Berkeley and Los Angeles: University of California Press, 1971), p. 140 and pp. 163–64.

particular. More seriously, to define oneself as someone's friend is often to remain unidentified for a secret purpose of one's own, as Radfoot and Riderhood do when they deceive John Harmon. The words "friendly" and "mutual" become downright sinister, in fact, when used to describe Wegg and Venus's pact, for their "friendly move" is a plot against Boffin. Similarly, the Lammles seal their marriage, a "mutual understanding," on the basis of getting back at the Veneerings. "Mutuality" thus seems inherently antagonistic to everything outside the mutual bond, but, more than that, "mutual friend" seems only another name for double agent. Venus, who betrays Wegg by working for Boffin, has good intentions, as does Harmon, but the idea of duplicity still makes one uncomfortable. It is as if duplicity is supposed to be morally neutral, suitable for purposes both good and bad. And the novel itself, giving away the Harmon/Rokesmith plot while keeping Boffin's ruse a secret, mirrors its characters' mutuality. Supposedly neutral, dialogically divided among his characters, the narrator plays his cards close to the vest.

It is the sense of having been taken in by the novel that accounts most of all for critics' unhappiness with its ending. Objections to Dickens's handling of the ending, based on a sense of having been unfairly treated, have prompted such responses as F. X. Shea's "No Change of Intention in *Our Mutual Friend*," which argues that Dickens did not change his mind about the plot at the very last minute. And after establishing intentionality, critics have proceeded to recuperate both the novel and themselves as readers. Robert Newsom, for example, shows how Boffin's fraud builds upon notions of fancy and authenticity in the novel, while Rosemary Mundhenk argues that Boffin's deception educates the reader.[14] Such readings, however, elide the emotional response which provoked them in the first place. Critics in general have either evaded or admitted failure in accounting for their feeling of

---

14. Frances X. Shea, "No Change of Intention in *Our Mutual Friend*," *Dickensian* 63 (1967): 37–40; Robert Newsom, " 'To Scatter Dust': Fancy and Authenticity in *Our Mutual Friend*," *Dickens Studies Annual* 8 (1980): 39–60.

having been wronged by the text. As Mundhenk writes of her own discussion:

> This argument . . . does not account for the reader's emotional reaction, his sense of being 'tricked.' There is a serious problem in the rather simple psychology of the 'pious fraud': having been shown his error, one is supposed to reform or convert. This strategy works with Bella, but it may not be so effective with a sophisticated reader. (50)

But it is the "sophisticated reader" that the novel both creates and undoes. Readers often characterize their response to the novel's ending as "disappointment," as in Grahame Smith's well-known remark: "One of the biggest disappointments in literature occurs in *Our Mutual Friend* at the moment when we discover that Boffin's moral degeneration has been nothing but a well-intentioned sham."[15] As a critical response, disappointment confuses self and text. Are we disappointed in the novel for misleading us, or in ourselves as readers for failing to perceive its design? The reader here bears an uncomfortable resemblance to Wegg, disappointed that "Our House" fails to match his idea of it. As I have shown, the moment of surprise engenders exactly this kind of confusion, revealing readers to have been inside what they thought they stood outside. And recuperative readings further ground the reader's narratorial, or "outside," position: in many cases critics discover, not very surprisingly, that they have "known" all along. Yet critical disappointment is grounded, or foregrounded, in the novel in ways which recall the notion of readerly identification Dickens so shrewdly invokes in Boffin's case.

For *Our Mutual Friend* establishes disappointment as an appropriate response to being misled. Indeed, the novel proposes misleading as an activity specifically designed for the purpose of disappointing. Disappointment, for example, is Silas Wegg's punishment for having plotted against Boffin:

---

15. Grahame Smith, *Dickens, Money, and Society* (Berkeley and Los Angeles: University of California Press, 1968) p. 182.

"Now, scoundrel," said John Harmon, ". . . I shall make two
more short speeches to you, because I hope they will torment
you. . . . you may know we knew enough of you to persuade
Mr. Boffin to let us lead you on, deluded, to the last possible
moment, in order that your disappointment might be the
heaviest possible disappointment." (859–60)

And "disappointment" is the term the Lammles use when
they discover after their marriage that—in Alfred Lammle's
words—"We have both been deceiving, and we have both
been deceived" (172).

But most significant, Dickens uses the physical representation of misleading to dramatize Eugene Wrayburn's knowledge of and power over Bradley Headstone. When, toward
the end of the novel, Headstone takes to watching Wrayburn
and following him at night in an attempt to discover Lizzie's
whereabouts, Wrayburn, aware of Headstone's watching,
watches him, and thus knows when he is being followed. He
then leads Headstone on aimless, frustrating chases.

> Having made sure of his watching me, I tempt him on, all over
> London. One night I go east, another night north, in a few
> nights I go all round the compass. . . . I study and get up
> abstruse No Thoroughfares in the course of the day. With
> Venetian mystery I seek those No Thoroughfares at night, glide
> into them by means of dark courts, tempt the schoolmaster to
> follow, turn suddenly, and catch him before he can retreat.
> Then we face one another, and I pass him as unaware of his
> existence, and he undergoes grinding torments. . . . Night af-
> ter night his disappointment is acute, but hope springs eternal
> in the scholastic breast, and he follows me again to-morrow.
> (606)

Wrayburn here deliberately both invites and evades what
might be a moment of recognition. But the reversal he has
already staged, with the reader's knowledge, and his toying
here with reversal underscore the potential reversibility of
narrator-character positions. Headstone, who begins as the
leader, ends up the follower. Wrayburn, whom Headstone
imagines to be a character in his narrative, has made Headstone a character in his. The scene dramatizes the moment of
surprise as a demonstration of knowledge by means of pe-

ripety, or reversibility. In so doing, it dramatizes as well the moment at which the text turns on its reader—or, we might say, looks at its reader, taking him or her by surprise—and readers who have considered themselves omniscient find that they have been misled, exposed, and taken in.

Conclusion

My purpose in the preceding chapters has been to defamiliar-
ize what is often considered nothing more than the Victorian
novelist's ordinary business: the construction of characters by
a voice claimed by no one and emanating from nowhere; the
exposure of what transpires in the minds of imaginary others;
the assertion of absolute knowledge about external and internal events. I have suggested that these and other phenomena
are not expressive of an assured possession of knowledge, but
rather of a fantasy of transcending character, of imaginatively
exceeding the boundaries that define individual identity by
inscribing them elsewhere. But, I have also suggested, even as
it makes knowledge of the presumably hidden seem available
and credible—even as it sees through rooftops—omniscient
narration cannot erase the traces which cause us to wonder,
after all, Who is speaking?

Dickens was a particularly apt subject for this enquiry for a
number of reasons. His novels and sketches repeatedly situate
fixed, circumscribed characters in opposition to presumably
unlimited, mobile, knowing narrators who create an effect of
omniscience by demonstrating their mobility and knowing-
ness to both characters and readers. His works contain figures
whose simultaneous identification with the perspectives of
narrator and character exemplifies omniscience's paradoxical
need to identify with character and at the same time remain
unconstrained by the limitations of any fixed position. And
Dickens's work is central to an understanding of what I have
described as the Victorian novel's circulation of privacy and
familial feeling: the way omniscient narration, by speaking for
"no one," insists upon the veracity and naturalness of specific
middle-class Victorian values.

It has not been my intention to restore presence to the narrator's place, nor to propose absence as an alternative to presence. My interest lies rather in the tension between self-effacement and self-assertion I see as characteristic of omniscience. By focusing on omniscience as a demonstration of mobility and knowledge, I mean to transform our reading of omnscience, so that a narrative mode that has traditionally signified an unquestioned assertion of authority may be understood instead to interrogate the grounds of its authority. And by representing omniscience as a form of narratorial hiding rather than an authorial disappearance, I mean to suggest that the omniscient gaze bears traces of the same personal and cultural identities it seeks to efface.

Though I rely on categories defined by narrative theory, I intend this argument as a corrective to narratology's classificatory tendency. The category of omniscience, and all such categories and names, offer useful starting points for analysis, but need not, I believe, be preserved in any particular form for the sake of a science called narratology. Indeed, I hope to have demonstrated that categories such as narrator, character, plot, as well as first- and third-person, are most interestingly approached as invitations to cross over the boundaries that traditional narrative theory attempts to establish—boundaries on which, as I have argued for Dickens's omniscience, I must rely if I am to demonstrate my ability to transcend them. Such categories may provide an opportunity to undo their own reification—their abstraction from the novels from which they are derived—by inviting us to read backwards, recovering the cultural conditions that produce certain narrative forms and understanding the assumptions underlying literary critical classifications of narrative. Recasting omniscience as construction rather than manifestation—as a fantasmatics of knowledge—I have suggested the congruity of narrative forms with other cultural and social systems. And considering omniscience as an effect of narrative strategies rather than as a collection of "points of view" which, when added together, yield a coherent authorial consciousness, I emphasize the idea of omniscience *as* effect: as an exchange between narrator, characters, and readers.

Omniscient narration belongs to a series of cultural phenomena through which the gaze—and, more generally,
knowledge itself—is coded as white, male, and middle class.
Since I have focused broadly on several of these issues, I want
here to elaborate further one form a discussion directed specifically toward the relationship between nineteenth-century
narrative omniscience and gender might take. The association
of omniscience with masculinity is occasionally taken up in
explicit terms in nineteenth-century fiction. In *Vanity Fair*, for
instance, Thackeray's narrator deliberately points toward the
male perspective of his omniscient gaze. In a voice not unlike
those of the old boys he satirizes, he remarks that "a man can
no more penetrate or understand those mysteries of female
fashion than he can know what the ladies talk about when
they go upstairs after dinner."[1] And, conscious of his narrator's implied gender in a way that Dickens never is, Thackeray
exploits omniscience's ability to "peep" into Amelia's bed-
room—now drawing the curtain, now putting it by, and delighting in his ability to do so. "I know where she kept that
packet she had—and can steal in and out of her chamber like
Iachimo—like Iachimo? No—that is a bad part. I will only act
Moonshine, and peep harmless into the bed where faith and
beauty and innocence lie dreaming" (154). And in *Shirley*,
Charlotte Brontë explicitly challenges the assumption of male
omniscience both when she allows female characters access
to knowledge from which male characters are excluded and
when she uses the novel's omniscience to expose the limitations of the choices her heroines make. Brontë associates unseen observation with female characters in particular and with
female character in general. When Shirley and Caroline observe the fight at the mill, for instance, their watching is
juxtaposed to male action. As Shirley says, "we shall see what
transpires with our own eyes: we are here on the spot, and
none know it—we stand alone with the friendly night, its
mute stars, and these whispering trees."[2] Women are useful as

---

1. William Thackeray, *Vanity Fair* (Harmondsworth: Penguin, 1968), p.
440. Subsequent references included in text.
2. Charlotte Brontë, *Shirley* (Harmondsworth: Penguin, 1985) pp. 334–35.

narratorial agents, Shirley implies, precisely because they are not empowered in other spheres—because, at least in this case, they blend in so well with nature. In all of Brontë's novels, it could be demonstrated, male and female characters battle for the possession of knowledge and the narratological power that accompanies it.[3]

But an opposition between "masculine" and "feminine" does not always coincide with one between "narrator" and "character," neither in a discussion of omniscience in general nor of particular authors. (Indeed, Terry Lovell makes a case for the "femininity" of Elizabeth Gaskell's omniscient voice, based on her narrator's sympathetic stance.)[4] A discussion of omniscience and gender would have to take such complexities into account, its usefulness resting finally on the extent to which it enlarges rather than simplifies our understanding of particular authors and their relationship to the social codes of the period. The kind of reading I have done throughout this study thus begins to suggest ways in which narratological, epistemological, and social structures can be found to reflect on, and to be embedded in, one another. Here, this method results in an articulation of recurrent patterns in Dickens's work which, I believe, sheds light on all these areas without positing any one of them as origin.

Omniscience as I have described it is not a unitary vision but a divided perspective, in which identification with an invisible authority is balanced against identification with the subject constituted by that authority. Constructing itself in relation to the idea of character it evades, omniscience is thus a primary means whereby the Victorian novel creates an effect of subjectivity—an effect that appears to readers, to quote Richard Sennett once more, as "identity composed of materials from within."[5] And yet in Dickens, perhaps more than any other Victorian novelist, the identities of characters seem

3. Susan Lanser discusses the commonplace association between women and first-person narration in traditional novel criticism in *The Narrative Act: Point of View in Prose Fiction* (Princeton: Princeton University Press, 1981).

4. Terry Lovell, *Consuming Fiction* (London: Verso, 1987), pp. 86–94.

5. Sennett, *The Fall of Public Man*, p. 9.

rather to be imposed from without. Character is represented as an imprisoning structure, the confines of which readers, identifying with the disembodied narrator, may be glad to escape. Like so much else in Victorian culture, the existence of such tensions—and indeed the surprisingly unexplored paradox of omniscience itself, as a voice that refers to no one—undermine the idea of a coherent and knowable self, a self fantasmatically represented in literary characters. For if such representations reassure as to the ultimate legibility and coherence of self, who—or what—is doing the describing? My focus on omniscience as a tension between inside and outside, or between presence and absence, emerges from a sense that what we call subjectivity is in fact constituted by such tensions, and that the desire to speak as no one—to imagine the self, at least temporarily, as not-a-self—deserves a place in the story of the nature and construction of Victorian subjectivity. And, happily for those who want to go on telling it, that is a story no single narrator is likely to finish.

Index

Aggression, authorial, 13, 155
Allen, Richard O., 53n.
Altick, Richard, 8n.
Ambivalence: of flâneur, 25; of human interest, 27, 28, 61; of observation, 23, 44, 88, 89, 125–26, 130; of *Sketches'* narrator, 10, 44, 160. *See also* Interest
Arac, Jonathan, 3n., 157n.
Aristotle, 153
Armstrong, Nancy, 79–80
Arnold, Matthew, 8, 45–46
Asmodean figures, 14–16, 18, 159. *See also* Character-narrators; Semi-omniscience
Asmodeus, 14, 80, 88, 102, 103
Auerbach, Nina, 78n., 94, 115n.
Axton, William F., 84n.

Bakhtin, M. M., 157
Barthes, Roland, 1, 23–24, 106
Baudrillard, Jean, 14
Belsey, Catherine, 129n.
Bender, John, 7n.
Benjamin, Walter, 25. *See also* Flâneur
Bentham, Jeremy, 3, 11–12, 40. *See also* Panopticon
Benveniste, Emile, 2, 59n., 114–15, 137. *See also* Object; Subject
Blain, Virginia, 144n.
Bleak House. See Dickens, Charles, writings
Booth, Wayne, 2, 93n.
Brontë, Charlotte, 18, 169–70. *See also* Gender
Brooks, Peter, 46, 84–85
Brown, Marshall, 5

Business: vs. busyness of Esther, 139–40; constructed along the lines of family, 87, 89, 100, 101, 107; of criticism, 45–46 (*see also* Arnold, Matthew); vs. idleness, 26–28; of managing feeling, 73, 74, 109–11; of novelist, 61, 107–11, 167; as pretense for observation, 27, 28; of sympathy, 43, 44; of Victorian novel, 77, 111; world of, 73, 74, 78–80, 87–89, 100, 101, 107, 109–11, 140. *See also* Feeling; Public Sphere

Caserio, Robert, 153–54
Chambers, Ross, 7
Character: construction of, 4–6, 11–14, 16, 19–21, 24, 25, 38, 42, 112–14, 167, 170–71; eccentricity of Dickensian, 14, 32–33; and habit, 30–33, 104, 122; legibility of, 17–19, 37, 119; as limitation, 11–13, 19–21, 24, 25, 55, 103, 118, 123, 132, 154, 157, 158, 162, 165, 167, 170–71; as marked, 13, 14, 29, 116, 118, 119, 142, 149; as material construct, 13, 14; vs. narrator, 5–6, 11–14, 19–21, 23–25, 29, 36, 43, 49, 112–18, 119, 121–23, 130, 131, 142, 149, 150, 154, 158, 165, 167, 170; narrator as personified, 3; as narratorial surrogate, 16, 23, 131; representation of, 13–16, 33, 103, 104, 113, 116, 123, 130, 132, 142, 160–62, 165, 171; and repetition, 14, 30–31; as type, 32–34. *See also* Character-narrators; Narrators

173

Compositor:	Keystone Typesetting, Inc.
Text:	10/12 Palatino
Display:	Palatino
Printer and Binder:	Edwards Bros.